Love to ~ Marilyn

Praise for *The Zippered Heart*

"Step into liberty through the rapscallion brilliance of Marilyn Meberg."

— PATSY CLAIRMONT
Author of *Mending Your Heart
in a Broken World*

"I am always amazed at the combination of humor and theological depth in Marilyn's writing. She has done it again in *The Zippered Heart*. This book addresses the tough issues that need to be brought to the light for healing rather than hidden in darkness and shame. These are bold words from a brave lady."

— STEPHEN ARTERBURN
Creator of Women of Faith conferences
and Founder of New Life Clinics

"This is one of the most honest, transparent books I have ever read. It comes from one of the most honest, transparent friends I've ever had. Marilyn drags our secret thoughts and fears out of dusty closets and brings them into the liberty of the light of Christ. I love it!"

— SHEILA WALSH
Artist, Author, Speaker

"For thirty years Marilyn's compassionate exploration of the human heart has amazed me. Now, with skill and tenderness she opens that heart for all of us to see how fearfully and wonderfully we are made. This is her finest book—deeply felt and beautifully written."

— LUCI SWINDOLL
Author, Speaker

"*The Zippered Heart* is classic Marilyn. With wit and wisdom, she focuses God's love on issues other writers are afraid to address, guiding readers to understand how Jesus' healing grace can mend broken hearts and restore fractured lives."

— BARBARA JOHNSON
Author, Speaker

"I read Marilyn Meberg's new book with an excitement I have seldom encountered in myself. This book will change thousands of lives, because it requires that we look so precisely at both the dark and the light sides of ourselves. Then it brings a kind of overflowing grace and forgiveness. As a psychologist with thirty-five years of clinical experience, I can say that this is one of the best books that I have read."

— NEIL CLARK WARREN
Author of *Finding the Love of Your Life*

"'We lost the experience of perfection but we'll never lose the expectation of it', says Marilyn Meberg. This is the essence of this colorful, literary, amusing, outrageous, revealing, delightful book. Marilyn causes us to look inside the recesses of our hearts and sift out the plunder and pretense that makes us fall short of being our best. You're invited to unzip your heart and repair the contents."

— THELMA WELLS
Speaker/Author, Women of Faith

"*The Zippered Heart* is a perceptive and sensitive examination of the 'war within' between our two natures. Using many humorous personal illustrations and drawing on her own courage to confront her dark side, Marilyn Meberg points us to the place of victory that is both practical and biblical."

— ARCHIBALD D. HART, PH.D.
Professor of Psychology, Graduate School of
Psychology, Fuller Theological Seminary

The Zippered Heart

Marilyn Meberg

W PUBLISHING GROUP™

www.wpublishinggroup.com

A Division of Thomas Nelson, Inc.
www.ThomasNelson.com

Published by W Publishing Group, a Division of Thomas Nelson, Inc., P.O. Box 141000, Nashville, Tennessee 37214.

Scripture quotations not otherwise noted are from The Revised Standard Version of the Bible, copyright © 1946, 1952, 1971, 1973 by the Division of Christian Education of the National Council of the Churches of Christ in the USA. Used by permission.

Other Scripture quotations are from the following sources:

The Message (MSG), copyright © 1993. Used by permission of NavPress Publishing Group.

The Holy Bible, New International Version (NIV), copyright © 1973, 1978, 1984, International Bible Society. Used by permission of Zondervan Bible Publishers.

New American Standard Bible (NASB), copyright © 1960, 1977 by the Lockman Foundation.

The Holy Bible, New Living Translation (NLT), copyright © 1996. Used by permission of Tyndale House Publishers, Inc., Wheaton, Illinois. All rights reserved.

Library of Congress Cataloging-in-Publication Data

Meberg, Marilyn.
    The zippered heart / Marilyn Meberg.
        p. cm.
    ISBN 0-8499-3702-7
    1. Self-disclosure—Religious aspects—Christianity. 2. Christian life. 3. Sin. I. Title.
BV4597.53.S44 M43 2001
248.4—dc21   2001046969

Printed in the United States of America

03 04 05 PHX 8 7

To Pat Wenger . . . the wind beneath my wings

W ithout the loving and consistent prodding of Pat Wenger this book would never have been completed. Thank you, Pat for your unflagging faith in the value of this project. Not only did you cheer me on, you insisted you could decipher my illegible handwriting, magically transfer it to the mysteries of your computer, and send it on its way to my editor. You are one in a million and my gratitude for your loyal support and friendship knows no bounds.

Contents

Part 1

The Divided Heart

Good Girl, Bad Girl

DISCOVERING OUR DARK
AND LIGHT SIDES

The venerable Mother Goose writes about one troublesome aspect of the human condition in her well-known little ditty:

> *There was a little girl*
> *Who had a little curl*
> *Right in the middle of her forehead*
> *And when she was good*
> *She was very, very good*
> *But when she was bad, she was horrid.*

As a child I heard that verse with a disquieting sense that there was a personal truth in it just for me—no one else. I had excessively curly hair and worried that if one misplaced curl in the middle of the forehead could bring on behavioral disaster for the poem's child, what in the world would happen as a result of the wild, myriad curls flung around my entire head? Was I doomed to a life of moral turpitude?

With the passing of time, my slightly neurotic child mind realized there was no link whatsoever between bad behavior and curly hair. Actually, it was Darlene Blington who verified that truth for me.

Darlene came from a very troubled home with a violently alcoholic father and a depressed, ineffectual mother. Although I was not allowed to go to her house to play (my parents were concerned for my safety), I watched her with the other kids at school. Not only did she use obscene language, but she was also aggressive, meanspirited, and unable to engage in even an hour of play without erupting in angry outbursts of hitting people.

Of greatest interest to me in my observations of Darlene was not her behavior, but her hair. I was delighted to note that it was straight as a flagpole. That settled for me the issue of straight hair versus curly hair as a moral predictor.

In spite of the comfort of settling the hair question, I was further relieved to learn at the age of five that the disquieting instincts I sometimes felt prompting me to do the wrong thing instead of the right thing were what the Bible calls sin and that there was a cure for sin, named Jesus. Also of comfort to me was my mother's assurance that I was not the only one troubled with a "sin nature"; every human being in the world is afflicted with that malady. I liked that I wasn't alone! (However, I was quite certain at that stage in my life that neither of my parents fell into the sin category. I simply could not imagine either of them deriving the pleasure I did from an occasional convincingly creative lie.)

What troubles me now as an adult, having come to terms with the shortcomings of idealized parents, is not the many failings to which most of us succumb, but the convincingly creative masks we put on those failings. Because it is too threatening to face our shortcomings, we outfit them with false fronts and tuck the truth away in an obscure corner of our souls, hoping it won't be noticed by others, including ourselves. If we can keep our "bad stuff" in the dark, we think that perhaps we'll be viewed as victoriously spiritual persons worthy of serving communion on Sunday or leading the deacon board in prayer on Wednesday night.

There is a problem, however, with disowning or denying the less than admirable parts of our being. If we don't learn how to deal with those parts, we resort to various defenses that shield us from the truth that needs to be addressed. As a result, we live our lives with guilt and a nagging fear of being "found out."

In my book *I'd Rather Be Laughing*, I talked about a construct I use to help me deal more effectively with those disowned parts of the self. I envision my heart as having a zipper down the middle. On the left side is all my humanness—those parts of me I'd like to pretend don't exist, such as my selfish thoughts or, at times, even murderous thoughts. (Incidentally, my murderous thoughts seem reserved almost exclusively for motorists who cut me off, slow me down, or simply get in my way. On more charitable days I exchange these murderous thoughts for my fantasy of the personally designed dashboard dart gun, which no one on earth has except, of course, for me. With a simple flick of a switch I could fire little darts into the tires of my offenders. This would necessitate the moving of their cars to the right shoulder of the road, where their tires would hiss themselves into total flatness. Smiling happily, I would speed on by.)

Not only do my selfish instincts nestle on that side of my heart, so too do anger, guilt, shame, and dishonesty (just for starters). Because these evils are so incriminating, I don't want to admit their presence. I'd far rather admit to the dashboard dart gun fantasy, which, when compared to my darker instincts, seems benign and much less threatening.

On the other side of the zipper, the right side, are my spiritual inclinations. From this side of my heart I draw my determination to behave in ways that are kind, unselfish, gracious—even able to discard the dashboard dart gun fantasy altogether. In other words, the right side reflects the fruit of the Spirit, which is mine because of the indwelling presence of the Holy Spirit.

The value of this construct for me is that when I fearlessly look into the dark corners of the left side of my heart, identify the sin, and claim that which does not make me proud, I am then able to submit it to the influence and power of the Spirit's healing power. My job is to be willing to cull from the reject pile all that I've denied and disowned.

Now, I realize that by dividing the "good girl, bad girl" sides of my being I may be accused of being a divided self. Matthew 12:25 states, "Every kingdom divided against itself is laid waste, and no city or house divided against itself will stand." James 4:1 calls the divided will "war in your members." Even mental health professionals speak persuasively about our need to integrate the "good" and the "bad" in ourselves. To fail to do so, they say, creates a split in the personality.

Of course the ultimate goal for spiritual and emotional well-being is that we can integrate the two sides of the heart and ideally eliminate the "war" in our members. Quite frankly, I don't think that integration is ever fully achieved. To fully resolve all war in our members would be to achieve a perfect state of being, which is, of course, impossible this side of eternity.

However, I believe with all my shaky heart that it is possible to lead lives with far greater peace and security than most of us ever experience. That peace comes from taking an honest look at everything on the left side of the zipper and refusing to deny the existence of the troublesome stuff in the lonely corridors of our heart's left side that inspires us to lie, cheat, lose our tempers, form and feed various addictions, and then wonder if God does or ever could truly love us.

The peace-producing, mind-boggling truth about God is that He does not live only on the right side of the zipper, where our better inclinations inspire good behavior. He lives also on the left side: sitting, standing, and moving amid all the stuff that embarrasses us, makes us feel ashamed, and causes us to believe we're spiritual failures. He invites us to join Him there that He might offer Himself as a power source for evicting those unwanted tenants from the property of our heart's left-of-the-zipper side.

My desire for you as you read this book is that you will be inspired to identify and examine the stuff that keeps you in a state of bondage. The liberating truth is that whatever we've disowned or been afraid to look at is not beyond the reach of God's healing touch. Perhaps even more amazing, there's nothing, absolutely nothing, that He is unwilling to touch or heal. How do we know that? Let me remind you of the apostle Paul's words in Romans 8:31–32: "With God on our side like this, how can we lose? If God didn't hesitate to put everything on the line for us, embracing our condition and exposing himself to the worst by sending his own Son, is there anything else he wouldn't gladly and freely do for us?" (MSG).

God is for us! He's on our side, even when it's the left-hearted side. If, by faith, we will believe that soothing and exhilarating truth, we can begin the life-changing journey of seeing and knowing ourselves as we truly are with the sure knowledge that God is not only there, but He also embraces us—no matter what our spiritual condition—and promises us divine enablement.

I want the pace for this introspective journey to be relaxed, non-threatening, and even fun. Though we'll deal with some heavy topics, I can write or talk myself into a coma unless I have a few giggles along the way. I'll do my best, however, to keep that personal penchant from being annoying. If I go over the top a few times, perhaps you will bear with me.

The next chapter will deal more specifically with that "everybody's-got-it" duality of human nature. Each of us has a dark side that can surprise us and even horrify us, as well as a light side that assures us we're pretty fine persons—and we hope to goodness someone's noticing!

Chat Room Possibilities

1. When you consider your own light/dark nature, what are your most obvious light side characteristics?

2. What are your most obvious dark side characteristics?

3. What is your method of dealing with the dark side characteristics, such as denial, lying, false fronts, etc.?

4. How can the zipper image help you sort out your behavior choices?

5. Do you think some people have more dark inclinations than light?

Everybody's Got It

RECOGNIZING
THE ZIPPERED HEART

The divided heart or the duality of human nature is one of those universal themes that has captured the interest and imagination of writers, philosophers, and theologians for centuries. Plato's *Symposium* suggested that each human being has a double to whom he or she was once physically attached and that because of this one-time attachment, humankind is never quite free from that duality. (Do you suppose that may have been what plagued the little girl with the curl in the middle of her forehead?)

More compelling perhaps is Shakespeare's *Hamlet*. The character of Hamlet has prompted more discussion than any other character in literature. When I taught college-level English, I loved assigning my students to read this play because once they got over their mind-set of "What does Shakespeare have to say to me in this century?" we had energetic and even heated discussions about our own tendencies to be first of one mind and then another.

I remember one particularly notable class discussion about the fact that the play had been described as a "grand poetic puzzle" because there appeared to be two Hamlets: one a gentleman who expressed himself in tender, unforgettable poetry; the other a barbarian who treated Ophelia with incredible cruelty, murdered Polonius, and then graphically described how he'd pile up his guts into another room.

Vincent, a virile, barrel-chested young man who had been the most vocal of my students in not seeing the relevance of studying Shakespeare, burst into our class ponderings with, "Hey, this guy is no poetic puzzle; he's a mixed-up dude just like me. I go all over the map sometimes, and I can tell you it isn't always a pretty sight!"

That candor brought a moment of quiet to the classroom until the young woman seated next to Vincent (who had confided to me her desire to date him although she couldn't seem to get his attention) purred softly, "Well then, we'll simply call you 'Sweet Prince.'" Grinning, Vincent replied, "Okay—as long as you treat me gently because, after all, I'm a poetic puzzle." (Incidentally, he never did ask her out in spite of my deliberately assigning a research project for the two of them. Apparently poetic puzzles don't yield to manipulations.)

An Inner War

Like Vincent, most readers feel extremely sympathetic toward Hamlet, even to the point of identifying with him. This shows Shakespeare's brilliance and his ability to tap into every person's awareness that our thoughts and actions not only vacillate, but "go all over the map sometimes, and . . . it isn't always a pretty sight."

C. S. Lewis once said, "There is nothing in literature which does not, in some degree percolate into life." In so doing, literature holds up a mirror to our true selves: our motives, behaviors, failings, triumphs, and heartbreaks. Interestingly, that literary mirror is rarely at variance with Scripture. Not only does Scripture discuss the divided heart, it tells us that God says, "Every inclination of his heart is evil from child-hood" (Gen. 8:21 NIV). Jeremiah 17:9 states with equal definitiveness, "The heart is deceitful above all things and beyond cure. Who can understand it?" (NIV).

If ever secular literature underscored the biblical truth of the depravity to which the human heart is capable, it is in Robert Louis Stevenson's *Dr. Jekyll and Mr. Hyde.* Most people are familiar with this novel, whether they have read it or not. The horror of Dr. Jekyll's double consciousness, which plays itself out in the person of Mr. Hyde's despicable deeds, seems to have been absorbed in our cultural consciousness.

Briefly, the plot of the book is that Dr. Jekyll is a benevolent physician who finds his ordinary life stifling, so he concocts a potion that he injects into himself. After that injection, he becomes an evil person with a brutal animal nature, known as Mr. Hyde. For a short time Jekyll is able to take a reversal potion and resume his good-person existence, but gradually his better nature weakens. When at last he is on the verge of being found out, he poisons himself and dies.

What is so chilling about this novel is that as Hyde gains increasing control of Jekyll's life, we recognize that Stevenson has given voice to our own fears of letting loose the monster within us—that part of us that is drawn to violence and evil. This novel describes with biblical accuracy the personality's inner war and the consequences of conceding victory to evil.

Jekyll's first experiences into the depravity of Hyde produces in Jekyll a welcome and delicious suspending of all behavioral restraints. With enormous elation he wallows in his other self. Like most people who rationalize, "I can quit anytime," Jekyll felt he could keep himself in balance with the knowledge that all he had to do was take the potion that reversed his duality and restored his good behavior in the person of Dr. Jekyll. However, Jekyll lost control after Hyde committed a senseless and brutal murder. From that point on, Jekyll was no longer able to escape the evil that engulfed him.

Paradoxically, we are uncomfortable with the consideration of the depths of evil to which we can sink, but at the same time, we listen to the little internal voice that claims, *That level of wrongdoing doesn't describe me. Yeah, I have my little hang-ups and temptations, but they aren't really all that bad. Quite frankly, I think Scripture is a bit harsh about the human heart.*

In spite of my early childhood recognition of at times preferring naughtiness to goodness, I never had a full sense of the biblical truth that "every inclination of the heart is evil" until I was in my late twenties. I was raised in a Christian home, went to a Christian college, married a Christian man, had two darling children, and taught a weekly Bible study in my home. I was, quite honestly, pleased with myself and figured God probably was too. It was into this emotional and spiritual environment on a sunny California morning that God injected a shocking revelation regarding my evil propensities.

It happened as I made a quick right turn from a busy street into a strip mall to pick up our dry cleaning. The entrance to this mall was one-way and the width of a single car. I screeched to an unexpected halt to avoid rear-ending a stopped bread truck blocking the entrance. As a result, the rear of my car remained partially in the busy street.

The driver of the truck sauntered around to the back of his vehicle, flung open the panel doors, and began counting the loaves of bread scrunched together on the bottom pallet. I couldn't believe it! Why didn't he move ahead, free the entrance, and *then* count his stupid loaves in front of the Italian restaurant where I assumed the bread was going to be delivered? Didn't he know that he was not only blocking me, but that he had also put me in danger of being rear-ended?

Granting him the benefit of the doubt before declaring him a moron, I gave a short honk. He ignored me. I honked again. Still he ignored me. I was dumbfounded. What was this jerk thinking, and why was he ignoring the precarious situation he had put me in? This time I honked aggressively. Slowly he turned around and, to my utter astonishment, lifted his right hand and waved his middle finger at me.

He then turned and started counting packages of English muffins.

Stunned and now angry by this crude and undeserved behavior, I yelled out the window, "Move your truck!" He slowly turned around and yelled, "Go ____ yourself!"

That did it! This godly woman sprang into action. Yielding to a primitive instinct that in seconds surged through my entire being, I gunned my motor and shot forward with every intention of sending him headfirst into the pile of bread packages in that truck. Within inches of hitting him, I slammed to a halt as I realized with horror that what I was about to do was kill him—as if being buried in bread wasn't bad enough for this guy!

Smitten by the realization of my murderous instincts and shaking at what I'd nearly done, I threw the car in reverse . . . but not before he brought his yeasty fist down on my hood.

As I peeled away from the scene of this almost demonic experience, I headed for home. Muttering and pacing through the house for several hours, I finally quit shaking. "Lord, I wanted to kill that guy! I've never felt those kinds of feelings in my life. I'm a dangerous woman—maybe I'm as deranged as he is. What is wrong with me?!"

Though it wasn't a comfort, God reminded me of all those incriminating Scripture verses about my inherent sinfulness and assured me, *Yes*, you, *Marilyn, have a heart capable of wiping out a severely dysfunctional bread man.*

What was so unnerving to me about that experience was that bursts of intense anger had never been part of my experience. No one yelled in my home as I was growing up, and certainly there was never any hitting. My husband, Ken, and I never even raised our voices to each other or the children. The most malevolent fantasy I'd ever entertained had been the dashboard dart gun. Where did that surge of violence come from? If arrested, would I have pleaded temporary insanity or inherent depravity?

Years ago, in one of his incomparable sermons, Chuck Swindoll cited a quote that he was kind enough to pass on to me. (He didn't know I was a potential bread man terminator.) The statement originated with the Minnesota Crime Commission:

> Every baby starts life as a little savage. He is completely selfish and self-centered. He wants what he wants when he wants it—his bottle, his mother's attention, his playmate's toy, his uncle's watch. Deny him these once, and he seethes with rage and aggressiveness, which would be murderous were he not so helpless. He is, in fact, dirty. He has no morals, no knowledge, no skills. This means that all children—not just certain children—are born delinquent. If permitted to continue in the self-centered world of his infancy, given free rein to his impulsive actions to satisfy his wants, every child would grow up a criminal—a thief, a killer, or a rapist.

Once again the secular world affirms biblical truth. In fact this statement sounds like a more detailed version of Scripture's statement: "Every inclination of his heart is evil from childhood."

The Divine Imprint

The reason we don't live with more social and moral chaos than we do is that responsible parenting teaches our little pagans impulse control, boundaries, the value of right behavior, and the consequences of wrong behavior. But in addition to parental and societal restraints, there is another reason we don't live in even more chaos than we do, a reason that doesn't seem to be taken into account by the Minnesota Crime Commission. In the words of John Calvin, "A sense of Deity is inscribed in every heart." Each of us is imprinted with the image of God. Scripture states we are created in His image whether or not we know Him personally. That divine imprint enables human beings to behave in ways that can be truly noble, self-sacrificing, and compassionate. That imprint also gives us the inherent capacity to make choices that are good and not evil.

I remember reading a newspaper account of one of those endearing examples of humankind at its best. A few years ago at the Seattle Special Olympics, nine contestants, all physically or mentally disabled, assembled at the starting line for the one-hundred-yard dash, with a relish to run the race to the finish and win. All, that is, except one boy who stumbled on the asphalt, tumbled over a couple of times, and began to cry. When the other eight contestants heard the boy cry, they slowed down and looked back. Then they all turned around and went back to where he'd fallen. Every one of them. One girl with Down syndrome bent down, kissed him, and said, "This will make it better." Then all nine children linked arms and walked across the finish line together. Everyone in the stadium stood and cheered.

We are touched and inspired by the behavior of these challenged persons because at their core, their most elemental instinct was to rise up as a unit to tend to the well-being of their competitor. We love to see their lack of concern for winning and see instead their commitment to caring. That we as human beings are capable of such selflessness is comforting as well as inspiring.

Wait a minute, Marilyn. It sounds as if you may be contradicting yourself here. You've made a scriptural case for the inherent deceitfulness and wickedness of the human heart and even owned up to your own seriously murderous instinct toward the bread man. Then you shared that sweet story from the Special Olympics depicting people's inherent motivation toward doing good. So what, then, do you do with the not capable of any good thing description in Scripture? (Every now and then I have these internal dialogues.)

That's a good question (whoever raised it) and one that needs to be addressed. Because we do have the divine imprint of God within us, human beings, redeemed or not, are capable of truly selfless and noble behavior. We frequently read heartwarming stories to that end in magazines and newspapers and see them on television as well. It is this very capability to do good that causes us to think we're really not all that bad. We can even take that thinking so far that we see no need of a Savior. After all, we know that Jesus died for sinners; yet we think that because of our good deeds and kind behaviors, the "sinner" label doesn't apply to us.

Mr. Hyde Redeemed

Personally, I thank God for showing me the "Mr. Hyde" that can rise up in me with such unexpected intensity. I need always to recognize that in spite of my capacity to do good things, I am equally capable of doing bad things. If I don't honestly face that which resides on my heart's left side, I'll never fully appreciate my need of a Savior. I will instead remain like the Pharisee in Luke 18:11–12 who proudly and publicly thanked God that he wasn't as bad as other, less "righteous" people.

Possibly you do not recognize a Mr. Hyde in yourself. Sure, you occasionally lose your cool, but never to the point of catapulting a bread man into his English muffin stash. In addition to that, the thought of an "other" identity that overtakes you and drives you to uncharacteristic behavior in the dead of night does not even remotely apply to you. You have all your ducks in a row, and they simply do not quack unless called upon.

That being the case, take a minute to shine a light into the depths of your interior being and consider the following scenario . . .

What might your response be to a lost job promotion that you felt you deserved? What if that promotion went to one of your friends? Would you genuinely congratulate her and promise your full support? Or would you find just the right person at just the right time to confide, "I hope this new job will not prove to be too much for _____. After all, she doesn't have a college degree, and her training is limited."

Suppose that, based upon the increased salary the promotion provided for your friend, she and her husband bought a new home with far greater square footage than you could ever afford. How would you respond? Would you congratulate her on her big new home, or would you drop comments like, "I sure wouldn't want to do the maintenance required for that huge house and yard"?

How would you feel when you learn the friend's husband wants a divorce because he has another woman in his life? That means the new house will need to be sold; your friend cannot maintain it alone. What would be your secret thoughts and emotions? Any sightings of a quiet Mr. Hyde?

We would be horrified if anyone knew the full extent of our envy, jealousy, and uncharitable thinking. Wisely, we try not to show that side of ourselves because it would be hurtful to others. Nonetheless, we know what we're hiding. What we hide and deny become our carefully guarded secrets. Those secrets may cloak full-blown Mr. Hydes or small, "human-nature" Mr. Hydes. Unfortunately, however, Mr. Hyde is alive and well in each of us, and we need to keep an eye out for him. We can usually find him seeking anonymity to the left of the zipper.

Scripture is consistent in pointing out the utter wickedness of the human heart so we'll understand that our good deeds are not good enough to meet God's standard of perfection. Isaiah 64:6 says, "All our righteous deeds are like a filthy garment" (NASB). The only perfect person who could measure up to God's standard was Jesus. He died for our sins that we then might be seen as righteous by God—not because of our good deeds, but because of Jesus' perfect sacrifice. If we place our faith in Christ, we are fully accepted by God because He sees us as having been totally cleansed and forgiven.

But even as a believer and receiver of Jesus, I occasionally need to be choke-chained into a realization of the depravity of which I am capable. Sometimes it's easy to forget that I am no more righteous in and of myself than one of the perpetrators of ethnic cleansing in a foreign country. That realization is what sends me to my knees, where I ask for forgiveness and then bask in God's grace, which assures me that I am no longer condemned.

Chat Room Possibilities

1. Do you think we all have a Mr. Hyde lurking about the left side of the zipper?

2. Have you ever had an experience that jolted you into a realization that your dark side is capable of doing damage?

3. Do you agree or disagree with the Minnesota Crime Commission's statement that every child "if permitted to continue in the self-centered world of his infancy, given free rein to his impulsive actions to satisfy his wants, . . . would grow up a criminal—a thief, a killer, or a rapist"?

4. Why do you think it is so threatening to truly see our dark side?

5. To what extent are you willing to examine your dark side? Of what benefit is that examination?

Behind the Curtain

OPENING THE DOOR
ON OUR SECRETS

In *A Tale of Two Cities*, Charles Dickens writes: "A solemn considera-tion, when I enter a great city by night, is that every one of those darkly clustered houses encloses its own secret; that every room in every one of them encloses its own secret, that every beating heart in the hundreds of thousands of breasts there, is, in some of its imagining, a secret to the heart nearest it."

I love the contemplation of the mystery and complexity of human-kind. People in close proximity may appear open and genuinely caring, yet there may exist in their demeanor that certain ill-defined something that signals me I can get only so close and then . . . they gently close the door. I found that true even with my own family members. My hus-band, Ken, was a very private person. His gregarious and charming manner implied easy access to his soul, but such was not the case. He was loving, kind, generous, and an utter delight, but much of his inner being remained a mystery to me. When he died of cancer at age fifty-one, I felt bereft of a full knowing.

The same was true of my mother. She too was warm and loving but private and reserved. Much of her remained "a secret to the heart nearest it." In contrast, my father was verbally open, emotionally accessible, and loved to talk at the level of intimate exchange. My personal inclinations about the secrets beating in the hearts of others and those beating within my own heart are to pour a cup of tea, pull up a chair, and chat.

Every human soul houses innumerable secrets. Every human soul has its own style in safeguarding those secrets as well as a different degree of ease with which those secrets are allowed to step out from behind the curtain.

One of the most fun parties Ken and I ever gave centered on a spontaneous comment he made early in the evening. He suggested that everyone tell a secret that was embarrassing, but not so humiliating that he or she would object if Ken shared it with everyone he met the next day.

There were two persons whose secrets sent us all into unexpected gales of laughter. The first was told by a quiet and conservative man who generally observed his environment more than participated in it. He blew us away with a recounting of how, in his senior year of college, he and his roommate rented a Cessna 182, stripped down to nothing but tube socks and tennis shoes, and then parachuted over their university campus. Because they drifted slightly off target, one touched down on the baseball diamond during the eighth inning of a well-attended game. The other landed on top of the administration building and was unable to escape without the aid of campus police.

The second favorite secret was told by a woman who had, with her husband, been a missionary in New Guinea for ten years. She said it is the custom among some tribes in New Guinea to greet a woman with a kiss on her bare left breast. With that information stated, she said no more. Ken asked, "What's the secret here?"

"Well, the secret is . . . I liked it!"

We all howled and clapped. Her husband's response was, "I wonder if that accounts for those easy conversions during our time there."

Probably the reason those two secrets were the party favorites was the secrets didn't match our perceptions of the secret holders. A conservative chemical engineer and a devout missionary allowed us to peek behind the curtain and glimpse their uncloaked humanity.

Handle with Care

Unlike the lightheartedness of those party secrets, many of us have learned that to reveal secrets can be disastrous and personally devastating. That was the experience of Sophie, countess of Wessex, who is married to Prince Edward, youngest son of Queen Elizabeth. She was recently caught in a sting of enormous proportions. A reporter for Britain's *News of the World* posed as a sheik and potential client for the services of the public relations firm of which Sophie served as chairman. With hidden cameras rolling, Sophie was videotaped gossiping about her royal relatives—additional possible marriages, the relationship between Camilla and Prince Charles and the unlikelihood of their marriage as long as Queen Elizabeth is alive, and how Sophie used her royal connections in ways that benefited her business.

That Sophie could stumble into such a royal mess came as a surprise because she, unlike Diana and Fergie, had until that time managed to avoid scandal. In fact, the media had considered her boring. She managed to change that image! Incidentally, she is no longer chairman of the board.

Not long ago, a young girl pulled a gun and opened fire in her school cafeteria. Another girl was shot and seriously wounded. Her offense? Telling the secrets of the shooter.

Our secrets are like porcelain: fragile and in need of careful handling. They can be fragments of our splintered selves, and we are wisely judicious before we risk placing them in someone's hands. That caution understood, what about the familiar refrains "We're as sick as our secrets" and "A secret has no power once it's told"? Is it healthy, wise, or necessary to share the deepest secrets of our hearts in order to free ourselves of the weight a secret can impose upon our souls? Is it not too risky to reveal those secrets that might damage our reputations if we dare to part the curtains?

Nathaniel Hawthorne's probing story *The Scarlet Letter* considers those questions through the characters of Hester Prynne and Arthur Dimmesdale. Hester was convicted of adultery by Boston's Puritan leaders; she gave birth to a child while serving her sentence in a local jail. Upon her release from prison, Hester was led to the town square, where she ascended a scaffold and, with her baby in her arms, suffered scorn and public admonishment. Condemned as an adulteress to wear a bright red letter *A* over her breast, Hester surprised the towns-people with her air of silent dignity.

She took up residence in a lonely cottage by the sea and came into town only when she had need of various supplies. Children jeered as she passed, other women avoided her, and clergymen pointed to her as a living example of the consequences of sin. Rumors circulated that she was a witch and that the scarlet letter she wore glowed a deep blood-red in the dark. Hester withstood the abuse without complaint.

Arthur Dimmesdale was a minister in the community who was deeply respected for his godly sermons and loved for his gentle, caring manner. Unknown to the community was the fact that he was the father of Hester's illegitimate child. He longed to confess his sin and resolve his intense sense of hypocrisy but was too afraid of the shame and ostracism open confession would bring. To make matters worse, the weaker and more guilt-ridden Dimmesdale became, the holier he appeared to his congregation. Every sermon he preached seemed to be more inspired than the last.

As the years passed, Hester, in spite of public disgrace and isolation, devoted her life to charitable service and won the hidden admiration of many of her peers. Dimmesdale, on the other hand, was increasingly weighed down by unbearable remorse even as his reputation for holiness increased.

One day, seven years after Hester's initial public censure, she came upon Dimmesdale walking through the woods at the edge of town. Speaking together for the first time since her trial and condemnation, Hester attempted to assure the minister that his good works and humility had gained him penance. But Dimmesdale cried out, "Happy are you, Hester, that wear the scarlet letter openly upon your bosom! Mine burns in secret!"

Because Hester's secret became known, she was not haunted by the fear of public exposure as was Dimmesdale. But in both cases there was great pain: Hester's public, Dimmesdale's private. In this instance perhaps the statements "We're as sick as our secrets" and "A secret has no power once it's told" hold true.

Actually, I think there is always a sense of relief that comes with a released secret. The issue is not *whether* the secret should be told, but *to whom* it should be told. I object to most public confession, which in my view tends only to deepen a person's shame and increase the potential of public ostracism. Unfortunately, very few people can be trusted to extend the grace that God so freely gives to His deeply flawed creations.

Whether or not to hold your secrets and protect them from public scrutiny is a matter of personal preference. As for me, I usually don't want to go public with my secrets, but I do want to select a few kindred souls who know me and know my unattractive and even appalling secrets. There is nothing more liberating than being fully known and still loved.

To Tell or Not to Tell

Paul Valéry, the early-twentieth-century French poet, expressed a lifelong concern with the interior drama of our conflicting selves. He said, "A man who is of sound mind is one who keeps the inner madman under lock and key." It is safe to assume that Valéry would advise against the sharing of deep secrets. His stance may be the safer one to take.

The problem with the safer stance, however, is that it is also the lonelier stance. When we withhold ourselves from others, we have no intimacy—only a superficial veneer that poses as a relationship. Superficiality is fine for such activities as seeing a movie, watching a tennis match, or going out to dinner. But when I want to connect at the soul level, I seek out the person who really knows me, loves me, and will share my life in all its rough and scratchy imperfections.

I have three completely trusted friends with whom I share my secrets. They know everything about me. Is that risky? I suppose it is, but time has proven these friends to be worthy of my trust. Time has also proven them to be available to me when I need more than a dinner companion. Because I choose not to live in emotional isolation, I believe I am far more enriched by the discreet sharing of my inner self than I am by remaining silent and unknowable.

Though I respect as well as honor anyone's right to manage secrets in a way that feels safe and maintains personal dignity, what troubles me about secrecy is this: Many, if not all, of our secrets embarrass us. That's why they're secrets. We hope and pray no one ever finds out about them. Undoubtedly those kinds of secrets are emblazoned with the bright red letters that spell out "SHAMEFUL." So where do we keep those secrets? Behind the curtain. To the left of the zipper. There they inspire such neurotic behavior as addiction, low self-esteem, mistrust, relationship dysfunction, depression, or eating disorders.

I'll give you an example of a secret that refused to remain behind the curtain. Three years ago I spoke at our Women of Faith conference about the masks we wear to cover the pain we feel. A woman came to my book table after I spoke and simply said, "My name is Becky. I'm a pastor's wife. I'm sick of my mask and I'm sick of my life." I wanted to grab her, hug her, and hear her story, but she disappeared into the crowd before I even had a chance to respond.

I don't know if she felt she owed me an explanation, but I was thrilled to hear from her several days later. She described a portion of her pain to me. Becky had been fighting depression most of her life and bulimia for ten years. Jim, her pastor husband, knew about her depression but knew nothing of her bulimia; she had managed to keep that a secret. He was preoccupied with the needs of his fast-growing congregation, and Becky wanted to be a support to him rather than a hindrance. She taught a large Bible study for women each week and was in continual fear of "losing it" in front of everyone. When I saw her briefly at the conference, she was struggling not to lose it there in front of the fifty women she had brought from that study.

What has happened in her life these past three years is rather phenomenal. I have her permission to share some of it with you. Becky felt strongly that were anyone to know her two major secrets, bulimia and depression, she would be a "stumbling block" to people. As a pastor's wife, her faith could be called into question. She felt deeply responsible to maintain a spiritually strong image for the sake of others. She also felt deeply ashamed. Why couldn't she get a grip? How could she keep living with a pressure that threatened to explode within her?

Sensing her husband's distancing from her, which she interpreted as indifference and potential abandonment, Becky broke down one evening (the one evening that week when Jim was home) and shared with him the secret of her bulimia. In great detail she described how she binged on ice cream, potato chips, doughnuts, cookies, and candy until she felt momentarily filled. Then she described the ritual of getting rid of it all by shoving her finger down her throat to bring it up. She told him about her self-loathing and her determination never to binge and purge again, only to find the cycle repeating itself over and over anyway.

As Jim held his sobbing wife, he was stunned at what he'd heard but also a bit angry. He too thought she should get a grip and felt she would be a stumbling block to others. He felt her faith needed to appear strong for the sake of those whose faith was weak. Their partnership in ministry was built upon mutual belief in the need to model God's sufficiency for everything in life.

They prayed together for Becky and asked God to enable her to take Him at His word and not succumb to the weakness of her flesh. Becky felt enormous relief that Jim now knew about her bulimia. She determined that night to "get a grip." They both determined that for the sake of others, Becky's bulimia must remain a secret.

As the weeks passed, Jim's preoccupation with church matters increased; Becky's determination to be strong diminished. Then, one Monday morning, her worst nightmare came true: She lost her grip in front of her Bible study. With wracking sobs, she confessed that she was a failure, that she suffered from severe depression, that she binged and purged at least three times a week, and that she could no longer pretend to be a model of spiritual strength. To her utter amazement, the words, "I have failed God, I have failed my husband, I have failed all of you, and I am so ashamed" were followed by a mass movement of seventy-five women rushing forward to engulf Becky in loving support. They held her, encouraged her, and pledged to be instruments of healing for her.

Based upon the experience and recommendation of one of those women, Becky flew to Remuda Ranch in Wickenburg, Arizona, where, with the reluctant support of Jim, she entered one of the finest eating-disorder treatment centers in the country. Remuda specializes in a Christ-centered approach to helping women walk through the painful process of becoming whole. Becky learned how the loss of her mother to alcoholism and the subsequent abandonment by her father had laid the groundwork for her depression and eating disorder.

During the four months Becky was in treatment, she heard from at least two or three different members of her Bible study every day. These women continued to love her and support her in ways she'd never experienced in her life. She felt accepted, valued, and free to be "weak." She also recognized the tyranny her secrets had held over her heart.

One of the biggest changes in Becky's thinking was to realize that she didn't deserve to wear the shame banner. Her depression had an environmental root; it was not a sin and it was not her fault. Her challenge was to face her issues and be healed from them. Her bulimia was not a sin either. It was one of the many expressions of all the childhood pain she had never resolved. At Remuda that process of understanding and healing began.

Becky is once again teaching her women's Bible study, but she now has a new vulnerability. The women who attend have a new vulnerability as well. The group now has an atmosphere of love and receptivity that invites the sharing of souls and the sharing of secrets. The faith-based support system modeled by Becky's group is rapidly spreading to other segments of the church.

Jim has come to realize that his inordinate concern with looking good for the sake of others has had more to do with his own needs than with preserving God's image. He was deeply invested in having others think highly of him. When Becky left for treatment, he was embarrassed by her. He is slowly coming to realize that his own veneer of competency covers a vast chasm of insecurity. Becky jokingly told him that if he could just whip up an eating disorder, he could also go to Remuda Ranch and work through all the "stuff" in his chasm.

Earlier in this chapter I asked the question, "Is it not too risky to reveal those secrets that might damage our reputations if we dare to part the curtains?" Becky's story illustrates she was able to get help only when her cover was blown through an inability to keep her own secret. Were it not for the parting of the curtains, Becky and Jim would both have continued their valiant efforts at maintaining their divided selves. Instead, they have grown personally and been healed in ways that encouraged the healing of others in their faith community.

Not only does Becky's story illustrate the healing potential of a secret shared, but it also illustrates that not all secrets hunched on the zipper's left side deserve to wear the shame banner. Shame inspired

Becky's behavior, but the shame itself was undeserved. You will find that shame and its resolution are major themes throughout this book. That's because I'm convinced that nothing keeps us from integrating the right and left sides of our hearts more than shame does. It's a toxic tenant that we'll need every creative plan we can come up with to evict.

In part 2 we'll coax a few more common secrets out from hiding and into the light of God's grace as well as our understanding so we can see how our behavior is being influenced by them. But first, let's take a look at what else might be standing in the way of our inclination to pull back the curtain.

Chat Room Possibilities

1. What is your style in safeguarding your secrets?

2. Do you agree or disagree with this statement: "A secret has no power once it's told"?

3. What is your opinion about public confession? Do you think this should be a practice in the church?

4. Have you ever been hurt by entrusting a secret to someone who later betrayed you by telling the secret? How has that experience shaped your level of openness with others?

5. Did you grow up with family secrets that were "not to leave the walls of this house"?

The Denial Defense

DEALING WITH DENIAL

Mary was a fabulous cook. This buxom blonde Irish woman first attracted the attention of the food-loving world in 1897 while working for a family in Mamaroneck, New York. Her piecrusts were delicate and flaky, her sauces subtly and inventively seasoned, and her dinner rolls light and flavorful. On that score her employer had no complaints. The problem was that after she had been in the kitchen just ten days, everyone in the household—everyone except Mary—came down with typhoid fever. As soon as the illness broke out, the new cook disappeared in the middle of the night. She was the infamous Typhoid Mary.

For ten years, Mary Mollan moved from city to city and job to job. She worked in private homes and restaurants in Maine, Massachusetts, and New York. Everywhere she went, typhoid invariably broke out within a week or two. At least fifty-three cases of fever, many of them fatal, were traced to her cooking. It was assumed that hundreds of additional victims were simply not identified.

Mary was a victim herself—a carrier of typhoid who spread the deadly germs but did not suffer from the symptoms of the disease. Unfortunately, Mary also suffered from a touch of insanity. When George Soper, a New York health official, first confronted her with evidence she was a typhoid carrier, Mary vehemently denied the charge and took after him with a carving fork. Soper fled in terror. After a dramatic chase with fork in hand, Mary was finally apprehended. It took five policemen to subdue her.

When Mary's story hit the news, she became an international celebrity. In Britain, *Punch* devoted an issue to poems inspired by her notorious cooking. Her fame brought her a boyfriend, a twenty-eight-year-old mental patient to whom she was married in 1909.

When Mary was ultimately released from the state hospital, it was on the grounds that she would never again be involved in the preparation of food. For months, however, Mary kept one step ahead of health officials and under a fake name took jobs in a Broadway restaurant, a Long Island hotel, and a fashionable sanitarium. She was finally located when typhoid broke out in Sloan Maternity Hospital. She was discovered in the hospital's kitchen cooking up a savory Irish stew and apple pie.

In spite of her adamant protests that she had nothing to do with the illnesses of her patrons, Mary was arrested. Still in total denial, she spent the rest of her life in confinement, reading and rereading Charles Dickens's novels.

Mary's story appeals to the quirky side of me. I especially love the image of her spending her dwindling years devouring Dickens. However, we see the common and potentially lethal pattern of denial in her behavior, in spite of the touch of insanity that lends spice to her life's account.

Saving Our Hides

Denial is a refusal to see what's really going on either within us or in front of us. At its core, denial is a carefully crafted lie we tell ourselves and others, hoping that the truth will not be discovered and that the lie will not be challenged.

The most familiar biblical act of denial was when Peter lied about knowing Jesus. Fearing for his life, Peter claimed he never knew Jesus. That's the whole point of denial: We fear for our lives, either emotionally or physically; so, to protect ourselves, we deny the truth. The truth would demand an acknowledgment and then accountability. The result can feel overwhelming and threatening, so, to avoid that, we construct a wall of denial and settle in behind it.

Some kinds of denial we could call the "saving-the-hide" version. That was Typhoid Mary's. She had to make a living. She was a great cook. The fact that she made people sick and even killed quite a few was of secondary importance to her. Maintaining a job was preeminent, so she continued to roll out the piecrusts.

The same version of denial was evident with Peter. While he wasn't trying to maintain a job (he could go back to fishing), he did feel compelled to "save his hide" from the threat of persecution or even death at the hands of Jewish leaders. He didn't want to die; he didn't think taking a public stand for the truth was an option for him. Denial was.

We can think of high-profile murder cases we expected would result in a guilty verdict simply because the evidence seemed conclusive. But with the steadfast denial by the accused and some brilliant lawyering, the accused was pronounced innocent. It looked like effective hide saving had occurred: another reason to think of denial as a friend.

The most troubling hide-saving denial that I've experienced personally had to do with my ruptured silicone breast implants. In case you're not acquainted with that bit of trauma in my life, here's some history.

Twenty-eight years ago, my neighbor dashed across the street to tell me she was getting a fantastic deal on silicone implants from the plastic surgeon for whom she worked. "But," I asked, "isn't his specialty noses? He fixes noses, not bosoms."

"I guess he wanted to branch out," my friend Mary replied. "Anyway, he took the training, he's certified and board-approved, and I'm losing my boy-next-door look in the morning!"

Having sported the boy-next-door look myself for as long as I could remember, I was envious. "So how come you're getting a deal, Mary? What does that mean?"

"Well, my doctor needs the experience, so I get the surgery at cost. He told me he would offer the same deal to a few of my friends if they were interested."

That evening I brought up the subject to Ken, who was mildly horrified by the notion of the "I'll-give-you-a-deal-while-I-learn-the-procedure" mentality. I pointed out to Ken that there was some similarity in the shapes of noses and bosoms and maybe it wasn't really such a stretch to leave the nose for the . . .

Ken was not convinced. But because I couldn't rid myself of the craving to sport curves instead of planes, Ken did some investigating about Mary's doctor and learned he had impeccable credentials, as well as an excellent reputation with other doctors. With Ken's reluctant approval, I had the breast surgery done by the nose man.

The results were exceedingly gratifying. Even Ken became an enthusiast of the procedure. (I must admit, however, that the flaring little nostrils at the base of each breast were a bit distracting . . . especially in cold weather or allergy season.) The reality is I had no problems with the implants at all. In contrast, a friend of mine paid a breast augmentation specialist four times what I did and had to have the surgery redone twice. The first time, one breast pointed slightly north and the other south. The second time they both pointed a little south. I told her she should have hired a nose man.

Many years later, I finally yielded to the persistent nagging of my ob-gyn to get a mammogram. (I had not had one in two decades; I was afraid that Gestapo technique might cause my noses to run.) With ill-disguised horror, the doctor showed me on a sonogram that both implants were ruptured and that my chest cavity was full of free-floating silicone. She told me to "run, not walk" to a surgeon for the removal of the mess.

Assuming that my task was merely to get the operation and return to boyishness, I was stunned to discover that my entire body was splattered with stray silicone—the greatest concentration being in the lymph nodes under both arms. In spite of the removal of the implants, recovery from all that toxicity has proven to be slow and at times debilitating. I want to make it clear that I am speaking only of my experience with silicone; there are those for whom there are no symptoms of toxicity. In fact, my friend (the one who veers slightly south) has had no other difficulty whatsoever.

As long as we're on the subject of breasts, I've simply got to share with you a hysterical line I heard Joan Rivers say on TV. When asked what her favorite physical feature was, she said it was her breasts. But then she added that at her age she has to wear open-toed shoes to show them off.

Okay . . . back to the subject of hide-saving denial. Prior to the removal of the implants I began experiencing all kinds of weird symptoms. It all started with a peculiar but persistent itching of the little finger on my right hand. The next day my left knee was itching, soon followed by an itching right knee. Ten days later, not only did my entire body itch, but I'd broken out in welts and red blotches. The only parts of me not afflicted were my neck, face, scalp, hands, and feet.

This was a brand-new experience! I have no known allergies to anything and, short of the chicken pox when I was nine, never had an itch or a rash. Yet I had become nothing more than a walking, talking, compulsively scratching red blotch! It became a way of life.

I asked my doctor if there could possibly be any connection between the ruptured implants, the seeping silicone, and my increasing physical symptoms, which by then included what I later learned was fibromyalgia. She superciliously told me there was no scientifically proven connection between silicone and immunological disorders. I asked why, if that were true, Dow Corning (who manufactured the implants) faced a lawsuit about silicone toxicity, lost the suit, and then had to declare bankruptcy. She didn't answer the question.

Well, I thought, *I don't want to crusade to raise the moral issue of breast implants and their potential damage to public health. I just want to get these toxic things removed and get on with my life.* But I didn't get on with my life at all. After the surgery, in addition to the blotches and hives all over my body, I experienced increasing and debilitating fatigue, muscle weakness, pain and swelling of my joints, hair loss, memory problems, and headaches. Still my doctor maintained her position that there was no proven danger from silicone and that my new diagnosis, "connective tissue and related disorders," originated from some other source. Good grief!

My dear friend Barbara Johnson huffed and puffed about all this and insisted I see a doctor in Newport Beach, California, who, she said, did not live in denial! After he saw me, this doctor's response was almost as emphatic as Barbara's. "Marilyn, it doesn't take a rocket scientist to recognize that your body is full of poison," he said.

Though the news was not good, I could have hugged him. I was heartened also to realize that he was far from alone in believing in the toxicity of silicone and its potential harm to the body. Were it not for the meticulous and conscientious research from scores of other doctors and scientists, Dow Corning would not have been brought to court with sufficient evidence for them to lose their case.

The most blatant hide-saving denial came from the implant manufacturers that knowingly denied the risk potential of their product. Here's an excerpt from the plaintiff's supplemental submission. (Sorry about the medical jargon.)

There is no dispute that silicone can cause an extensive cellular reaction in many implanted women which results in chronic and granulomatous inflammation, granulomas, massive angiofibrosis, lymphodenopathy, capsular contracture, fat neurosis and tissue atrophy and the activation of secretory macrophages which release pro-inflammatory cytokines. . . . The manufacturers' submission did not dispute these adverse consequences. Instead, they attempted to downplay the significance of the cellular reaction to silicone by characterizing it as a "normal foreign body response" which is "part of the normal healing process."

Does this remind you of the tobacco companies who "downplayed" the risks of smoking? Talk about denial!

As far as my health is concerned, my hair is back, my energy has returned, and my skin is clear. I still have joint pain and think seriously before ascending a flight of stairs. I don't know what the long-term consequences will be for me, but as of this moment, one year later, I thank God for restoration I had not anticipated so soon.

Friend or Foe?

You may be tempted about now to say, "Marilyn, I don't think you're really talking about denial here. I think you're talking about lying." And you're right. I have been talking about lying. That's the core component of denial. All denial is fabrication. People in denial create a literal fantasy mind-set that they use to protect themselves from the truth.

For example, consider the mother whose son is repeatedly arrested for drug use. Her denial response is to claim that the police are targeting her son unfairly; after all, he's just a kid who occasionally "does his thing." She's lying to herself. What about the husband whose alcoholic binges are covered up by his wife, who is in denial? She admits that, yes, her husband drinks, but his consumption isn't excessive. She calls his boss repeatedly with various excuses of why he can't come to work. When the children cower in terror over his alcoholic rages, she assures them, "Daddy really loves you and doesn't mean the things he says." She's lying to the boss, she's lying to the children, and she's lying to herself.

I counseled a man whom I'll call Carl whose wife was obviously involved in an affair. She came home late, took occasional weekend trips, became withdrawn, and was emotionally and physically unavailable. The reason Carl came to see me was that his wife "didn't seem to enjoy him anymore." He wondered what he could do. He didn't think she could possibly be having an affair because, for one thing, she was a Christian, and "it would never occur to her to be unfaithful." Carl was lying to himself. Time and bitter experience proved his wife was indeed having an affair.

Is it a bit crabby to keep talking about denial as lying? What about those persons who have no idea they're in denial? It's almost as if they've had their memories wiped out. Can they be described as liars?

It is true that denial is a powerful defense against traumatic pain and that to live in or even remember that pain could overwhelm the senses. In that case, the denial defense mechanism kicks in and is a friend of sorts, a protector. Nevertheless, that denial is still about avoiding the truth; and if ultimately that truth is not acknowledged, looked at, verbalized, and the emotions connected with it felt, denial prevents healing the original pain. Denial then ceases to be a friend.

I'm going to seemingly digress for a minute and tell you an anecdote a radio talk-show host told that gave me a giggle. Hopefully it will illustrate my next point.

The doorbell rang and Clyde, the homeowner, opened the door and looked out. No one was there. As he was getting ready to close the door, he saw a snail on the doormat. Bending down, he scooped up the snail and flung it into the bushes adjacent to the driveway and then slammed the door shut.

Two years later, Clyde's doorbell rang. Looking out, he saw no one. As he started to shut the door, he looked down and saw a snail on the doormat. Before Clyde could slam the door, the snail shouted, "What in the world was that about two years ago?"

Whether you share my amusement over the rejected snail, here's my point: Sooner or later, whatever experience we've flung into the shrubbery in an effort to deny its existence will come back and ring our doorbell. It may take years, but it will come back. Of course, when that pain is flung into the shrubbery of denial, it will not return in its original form. Unlike the snail, which dared to come back exactly as it was the first time around, our disowned, denied stuff will come back in disguise. It can take the form of depression, anger, moodiness, irritability, or an inability to focus or maintain concentration. Any one of these symptoms points to the need to deal with the denied stuff that's ringing our doorbell.

Let me illustrate further by telling you about Teddy Montana. Teddy got his driver's license six months before I did, and my jealousy knew no bounds. He taunted me continually with comments like, "Hey, Ricker, still riding your bike, still walking to school. Need to be with someone who can drive?" Though he was a pill, I liked him a lot and considered him a good friend.

One morning on the way to school, Teddy and his friend Jack were broadsided by a car going about forty miles an hour. The driver of the other car had run a red light and smashed into Jack's side, killing him instantly. Teddy was badly bruised but otherwise escaped injury. His car was totaled.

Teddy's parents assured him he was in no way at fault (and he wasn't) and urged him not to let the accident ruin his life or "get him down." Their advice was to get on with high school and put the experience out of his mind. He did just that, and in a short time he managed to deny he'd ever had feelings of terror, guilt, and loss. His parents bought him a new car and expressed hope that he could once again be the happy-go-lucky kid he'd always been.

When gradually over the months Teddy's personality changed drastically, we were surprised and ultimately put off. He was rude, short-tempered, and often got into fights at school. Ultimately, he was kicked off the football team because of repeated alcohol use.

There was much less education about psychological issues in those medieval times than is available to us now. No one seemed to know what was wrong with Teddy except that his friends no longer wanted to be around him. Now, of course, it's clear that Teddy denied crucial emotions that needed to be vented, understood, and resolved and instead threw them into the shrubbery with the fervent hope that those discarded emotions would not creep forward and ring the doorbell.

Psychologists claim that denial is the unconscious repudiation of some or all of the meanings of an event in order to avoid the pain that event might trigger. Perhaps the phrase "unconscious repudiation" may imply we're off the hook. After all, we have put "it" all into the unconscious and truly don't know what was put there; it's beyond our conscious control. But that logic won't work. Here's why.

Pain, when denied, always results in maladaptive behavior: substance abuse, addictions, depression, inexplicable outbursts of hostility and rage, inability to maintain healthy relationships, ad infinitum. That behavior is known and seen; it is observable. It is destructive to the self as well as to others. We may not understand the reason behind these actions, but we can't claim the behavior is invisible.

Now when those actions are denied and kicked into the shrubbery— the property on the heart's left side—when we refuse to acknowledge them or examine their source, then our denial is not a friend that protects, but a foe that destroys. If we deny the stuff is there, we feel better about ourselves and are convinced we look better to others. But the problem with that denial defense is that we never deal with the junk. That means the left-hearted pile simply gets higher and higher and our behavior more and more out of whack.

Matthew 20:30–33 describes two blind men who were sitting by the side of the road when Jesus passed by. Responding to their shout, "Lord, have mercy on us, Son of David!" Jesus asked them what they wanted from Him. Their response was, "Lord, let our eyes be opened!" That needs to be the cry of all of us. The first step out of any form of denial is to see. When we see, we're no longer in denial. When we're no longer in denial, we're able to see the truth. The truth, Jesus promised, will set us free. Free from what? Left-hearted lodgers.

So, dear ones, as my grandmother used to say, "Let's get down to tin tacks." (I never understood what that expression really meant except that it sounded serious.) God is with us and He intends to heal us. That is serious as well as exciting!

Chat Room Possibilities

1. Do you agree that denial is a form of lying?

2. How has denial been a friend to you? How has it been an enemy to you?

3. Do you think all people live with a level of denial? Give some examples.

4. What have been the consequences of your denial?

5. What has been your reward for coming out of denial?

Part 2

Left-Hearted Lodgers

I'm So Ashamed

DEFEATING OUR SHAME

Why is it so hard for us to admit we are all at times living, breathing, left-hearted people? There are a few of us who fight against that admission with such strength and energy we could be likened to the cat who refused to take its pill.

A friend of mine took these instructions from the Internet and passed them on to me. Just in case you missed them, I'll share this bit of pertinent wisdom with you.

Instructions for Giving Your Cat a Pill

1. Pick cat up and cradle it in the crook of your left arm as if holding a baby. Position right forefinger and thumb on either side of cat's mouth and gently apply pressure to cheeks while holding pill in right hand. As cat opens mouth, pop pill into mouth. Help cat to close mouth and swallow.

2. Retrieve pill from floor and cat from behind sofa. Cradle cat in left arm and repeat process.

3. Retrieve cat from bedroom and throw soggy pill away.

4. Take new pill from foil wrap; cradle cat in left arm holding rear paws tightly with left hand. Force jaws open and push pill to back of mouth with right forefinger. Hold cat down for a count of ten.

5. Retrieve pill from goldfish bowl and cat from top of wardrobe. Call spouse from garden.

6. Kneel on floor with cat wedged firmly between knees, holding front and rear paws. Ignore low growls emitted by cat. Get spouse to hold cat's head firmly with one hand while forcing wooden ruler into mouth. Drop pill down ruler and rub cat's throat vigorously.

7. Retrieve cat from curtain rail; get another pill from foil wrap. Make a note to buy a new ruler and repair curtains. Carefully sweep shattered figurines from mantel and set to one side for gluing later.

8. Wrap cat in large towel and get spouse to lie on cat with its head just visible from below spouse's armpit. Put pill in end of drinking straw, force cat's mouth open with pencil, and blow down drinking straw.

9. Check label to make sure pill not harmful to humans; drink glass of water to take taste away. Apply Band-Aid to spouse's forearm and remove blood from carpet with cold water and soap.

10. Retrieve cat from neighbor's shed. Get another pill. Place cat in cupboard and close door onto neck to leave head showing. Force mouth open with dessert spoon. Flick pill down throat with elastic band.

11. Fetch screwdriver from garage and put door back on hinges. Apply cold compress to cheek and check records for date of last tetanus shot. Throw T-shirt away and get new one from bedroom.

12. Ring fire department to retrieve cat from tree across the road. Apologize to neighbor who crashed into fence while swerving to avoid cat. Take last pill from foil wrap.

13. Tie cat's front paws to rear paws with garden twine and bind tightly to leg of dining table. Find heavy-duty pruning gloves from shed. Force cat's mouth open with small wrench. Push pill into mouth followed by large piece of filet mignon. Hold head vertically and pour half-pint of water down throat to wash pill down.

14. Get spouse to drive you to emergency room; sit quietly while doctor stitches fingers and forearm and removes pill remnants from right eye. Stop by furniture store to order new table.

15. Arrange for vet to make a house call.

If you've lived to tell your own experience in medicating a pet, you could conclude that this instruction list is not far from the truth. In addition to giving me a giggle and pulling up childhood memories of my perennially depressed cat, Jeremiah, I find myself identifying with that feline resistance. Now of course I'm too civilized to hiss, spit, and break furniture, but there are certain left-hearted inclinations I don't want to accept, and I don't want anyone else addressing my need to accept them either.

For example, last summer a friend drove down to my rented Balboa Island beach house for a day. Our plan was to walk to the village for lunch, come back to my house, change clothes, grab the beach umbrella, and then luxuriate for the rest of the afternoon on the sand.

As we headed out the door for town, I dropped the house key in the back flap of my beach chair, which leans against the wall on the front porch. My friend paused and said, "Don't tell me you're leaving your house key there!"

"Yes, I am! I always pop it in that chair flap. That way I don't have to rummage around in my purse looking for it when I come home."

"Well," she said, "it doesn't seem wise or safe to me, but of course that's none of my business."

Finding her words mildly irritating but also thinking she might be right, I put the key in my shirt pocket instead of the chair flap. I also remembered why I only saw her a few times a year.

Finishing lunch and a very one-sided conversation where I learned everything she had done, said, or thought in the last seven months, we returned home, changed clothes, and started for the beach. On the short walk there she said, "Now, you have your key, don't you?" Attempting to keep my claws retracted, I said, "Of course I have my key—it's in the flap of my beach chair!"

After another two hours of one-sided conversation, she announced how much she loved our chats but simply had to head for home. As we climbed the stairs to my front door, I attempted to find the house key in the side flap of my beach chair. In frustration I threw down the umbrella, pole, and all the other stuff in my hands and on my back to better free myself for the key search. (Wouldn't you think she could have carried something?)

"Don't tell me you've lost the key," my friend said.

Trying hard not to hiss, I said, "Of course I haven't lost the key; I transferred it from my pocket after lunch. I distinctly remember putting it here—just give me a minute."

"You obviously did not transfer that key, or it would be there!"

"I most certainly did transfer the key. Maybe it fell out on the sand."

Rolling her eyes in exasperation, my friend trudged back with me to our "spot" to comb the sand with our fingers. No key. We walked back home.

A sweet guy painting a house across the street lugged his long ladder over to my second-story unit and insisted that he, not I, scamper up the ladder and walk through the open French doors (another safety infraction according to my friend) that led to the front entrance. As we walked in, I sheepishly thanked him and with relief saw my friend to her car. As she was driving away, her parting shot was, "Better call a locksmith, Marilyn, and then, for goodness' sake, take better care of your key!"

Pleased that I had not yielded to the instinct to claw her face, I ran up the stairs and down the hall. Grabbing the blouse I'd worn to lunch, I checked the pocket. There was my key! Contrary to my vehement insistence, I really had not transferred the key to my beach chair's flap. My friend was right. I hated that! She was overbearing, self-absorbed, and demeaning; she did not deserve to be right!

All evening I hoped she wouldn't phone to see if I'd called a locksmith. All evening I determined I would not admit to her that the key was in my pocket just as she had said it was. I even fabricated a great story about having returned to our sand spot where I met a wonderfully handsome, middle-aged man who compassionately helped me search through the sand and who found the key. We celebrated by having an intimate dinner later that evening. Carrying my fabrication even further, I imagined how he'd told me over dinner about the tragic death of his wife ten years ago and that I was the first woman he'd met since then who made him feel perhaps there was another love for him in the future. It was such a fun story, but of course I couldn't actually tell it to what's her face; after all, it was a complete and thoroughly compelling lie!

She called the next morning; I confessed. Her only comment was, "You really shouldn't live alone, Marilyn." Meow!

A Core Indictment

Admittedly my former friend's attitude was not attractive, but what was *my* problem? Why should I so resist admitting the truth to her? It is of course always easier to be candid when the atmosphere is supportive and warm, but so what? The bottom line was I didn't want to be caught being wrong! Why? Because being wrong chips at my self-esteem; I look better to myself (and, I assume, to others) when I'm right. I don't look good when I'm wrong.

Where did those thoughts come from? From the internal nagging moral tracers that extend all the way back to the Garden of Eden. Disobedience of God's law started there with Adam and Eve, and we've been ashamed of ourselves ever since. The moral tracers cause us to be aware that we're not living up to what we were originally created for, which is perfection. We lost the experience of perfection, but we'll never lose the expectation of it. We think somehow we'll get it back if we just work a little harder.

In the meantime, we hope no one will notice the full scope of our imperfection. We come up with elaborate cover-ups to divert attention from our true state—diversions such as the delicious lie about the man who found my key and found me so incredibly charming that he thought true love might enter his life again. Now that's a little pathetic, if you ask me. But I salve my embarrassment at even thinking up that whopper in the first place by telling myself that at least I didn't actually tell the lie. Maybe there's hope for me. Hope for what? Perfection? No way.

The reality is I'm not perfect. Surprise! I misplace my house key, I let people down, I try to look better than I am, I don't always do what I say I'll do, I sometimes betray confidences, and on occasion I've been known to fudge on the truth. Am I proud of this short list? (I've got a longer one.) Of course not. I am, quite frankly, ashamed of myself. And that brings us to the whole point of this chapter. (Finally!)

The reason it is so hard for us to admit to the "stuff" on the left side of our hearts is that we're ashamed of it. We think that if we keep denying our ugly stuff, then maybe we'll look better than we fear we actually are. But no matter how we scramble in our efforts to look good, we still suffer from a deep-seated sense of shame and will do almost anything to avoid that sense. Shame is not what we do; it's whom we perceive ourselves to be. Shame is a core indictment of our very essence.

The subject of shame has occupied the minds and writings of mental health professionals for the past few decades. As a result, many books and articles help us understand why our shame feels so shameful. Perhaps most helpful to our understanding is that at the very core of shame lives the panicked fear of abandonment and rejection. If you really knew me and the nature of the stuff that lives on the left side of my heart, you'd not only be shocked, but worse yet, you'd be appalled. If you're appalled, then I have every reason to assume you will reject me. If you reject me, I will experience abandonment, which is the most devastating emotional state in which to live.

One of the greatest driving forces of our nature is to feel connected to other human beings. To truly experience connection is to experience oneness; without it, we can withdraw into a world of lonely isolation. To avoid isolation, rejection, and abandonment, we deny our left-side realities; they are simply too threatening to acknowledge.

I do have to point out, however, that in spite of shame's potential toxicity, not all shame is unhealthy. The capacity to feel shame is normal, adaptive, and a requirement for developing healthy guilt, a sensitive conscience, compassion, and empathy. Healthy shame develops in an environment that is basically loving and nurturing. Were it not for healthy shame, we would not be driven to our knees in recognition of our need of a Savior. We wouldn't lift our voices then in praise and gratitude for the forgiveness of sin and the grace that says we're cleansed. But when shame becomes an identity, a state in which we feel different, despairing, and helpless, it then creates an interior environment in which the balance is lost between the healthy shame and unhealthy shame. This kind of unhealthy shame indicates that we've lost our true identity and value as God's creation whom He called into being out of love and with pleasure.

51

Can we blame our shame inclinations totally on the loss of perfection in Eden? No. Adam and Eve's sin was the root of our imperfection, but there are many layers that are laid on top of that foundation of original shame. Although there are many contributors to those layers of shame, they are usually laid first in childhood.

The Building Blocks of Shame

I believe most parents who have contributed shame to the junk pile of their kids' hearts have done so unwittingly. Without realizing the intense ramifications their words or actions may have upon the developing sense of self, parents can unintentionally do long-lasting damage.

When parents communicate to the young people in their home that they are loved and appreciated, those children assume then that they are valuable, worthy members of the family. That assumption translates into feelings of self-esteem so they do not find it hard to fathom they are lovable. For example, regularly using phrases such as, "I love you," "You are wonderful," "I am proud of you," and "You give me joy"—with accompanying hugs and kisses—builds a secure environment in which shame is rarely, if ever, experienced. When the child misbehaves and needs to be corrected, discipline can still be handled in an atmosphere of positive and unconditional love. Hopefully, the parents communicate that certain behaviors are unacceptable, but never the child.

Sadly, however, many children rarely, if ever, hear the words, "I love you" or "I'm proud of you." The parents may feel love for their child and may even be proud of her, but if the words are never spoken, the child does not experience affirmation. That lack produces insecurity. This kind of environment causes the child to think maybe she isn't lovable and maybe she is nothing to be proud of. Those thoughts open the door to shame—the private, core evaluation of the self.

I have a dear friend who was rarely hugged and, to her memory, never praised her entire childhood. Her parents were well-meaning, basically nonverbal people who worked hard but had no idea how to communicate acceptance or love. The result is that my friend, now as an adult, never feels satisfaction with the quality of whatever she does. She continually berates her writing, her speaking, her ap-pearance, and her value to her profession. There is always a little voice in her head that says, *You could do better, others write far better than you, and if you're going to be a public speaker, you'd better learn to express your-self more effectively.* The clincher message she hears in her head is, *You ought to be ashamed of that sloppy performance!*

That feeling of not being good enough carried over into her mar-riage. She's sure her husband must be disappointed with the kind of wife she turned out to be. According to her, he's too nice to say so, but in her heart she believes he wishes he'd never married her. That belief about herself was further underscored by the fact that she has not been able to have children. There doesn't seem to be a medical reason for the childlessness, but my friend is sure it's her fault.

Children initially have no measuring stick to use in determining their value except the reactions they get from their parents. Unlike the parents in the previous example, some parents are exceedingly verbal with their children, but their verbalizing is negative and critical. "If you can't say something nice, don't say anything at all." "I can't believe you haven't at least brought that reading grade up from a C. Your sister never got a C in her life. I guess it's obvious who has the brains in this family!" "You've got the worst-looking hair I ever saw—maybe we ought to just shave it all off!"

Some of the ways we produce a lack of personal worth and value (shame) in our kids are more subtle than the previous examples but never-theless damaging. Children can be made to feel like a burden, an intru-sion, an irritation, or an inconvenience—even if the words are never spoken. Such messages can be communicated through repeated expres-sions of impatience and exasperation or by phrases like "I just don't have time" or "Please don't bother me right now; I have so much I need to do." To my utter chagrin and deep regret I used the phrase "I just don't have time right now" far too many times as our two children were growing up. As I look back, I have no memory of what great deeds I accomplished with my insisted-upon time, but I have a vivid memory of their disappointed little faces.

When parents have no time and are impatient and exasperated, they've planted shame seeds. If they seldom praise, frequently criticize, and rarely hug their child, the child's shame flourishes rapidly. And when the child is made to feel like a burden instead of a pleasure, the shame, like a creeping vine, trails her through life.

The bottom-line assumption made by any child who experiences these environmental lacks is that the problem lies with her, not the parents. The child, based on the evidence, simply decides she's a disappointment, a mistake, maybe even a total loser! If she's an inherently spunky little kid, she'll fight the messages and try to disprove them by concentrating on her performance, trying desperately to be the best in whatever. Let me give you an example.

In my first year of teaching, I had a classroom of especially macho third-grade boys with equally macho third-grade girls. I frequently wondered if the water supply in that neighborhood had been spiked with heavy doses of testosterone. I didn't know how else to account for their hurly-burly ways. What gave me a giggle was the fact that there was no bullying of the girls either on or off the playground. The boys knew that if there was just one unwanted behavior from any one of them, the girls would simply deck him with one flashing fist to the jaw, step over his sprawled body, and continue playing jump rope. The result of all this was a very peaceful playground as well as classroom. (Ken suggested that rather than drink the water at the school during breaks and the lunch hour, I might want to take my own bottled water. I think he feared what I might become.)

Several weeks into the year, a new boy arrived from Mexico and was placed in my class. He spoke a little English and I spoke a little Spanish; the result was a fun series of gestures and drama. He told me his name was William. I foolishly called him Billy several times, I guess in an effort to establish greater familiarity. Whatever the reason, William began signing all his papers Billy William. He became Billy William then to everyone.

What concerned me about Billy William from the first day was the obvious lack of testosterone he exhibited. I worried his pudgy little body might become a target for my third-grade cave men and women the minute they all hit the playground. I was stunned to find how ill-founded my fears were. I watched during dodge ball in the morning, kickball at noon, and baseball in the afternoon, while Billy William tore around the playground as if he'd been goosed by an electric prod. He ran faster, dodged more adroitly, and hit the ball farther than any of my little Neanderthals.

Curious to know what drove this little dynamo, I told his mother during our first parent-teacher conference that he was the best athlete in my class. She laughed and said, "No, no, not William; he a runt." I asked if there were other children in the home. "Oh yes: Pedro. Pedro big; Pedro smart; Pedro run and run and run."

The next day I asked Billy William about Pedro. Billy William's eyes lowered to his paper and then he whispered, "Pedro best."

I bent down and whispered, "I think Billy William's the best. He's fast as a racecar!"

Billy smiled slowly. "Yeah . . . racecar!"

From then on I no longer called him Billy William: I called him Racecar. He was soon signing his papers Racecar. And before long, my little Neanderthals were calling him Racecar as well. (Poor kid—I may have built his esteem, but he lost all name identification.)

As I attempted to envision the dynamics of his home life, it seemed safe to assume William was called "Runt" and probably received little recognition. It appeared that Pedro was the family hero; William was merely a presence. But rather than hang back and accept "runt" status, William rose up determined to be better and faster than a runt.

Lots of kids manage to compensate and seemingly cancel out negative messages by excelling in various endeavors. Those are the kids with pluck and grit who refuse to be discounted. Even so, they're never sure they're good enough and often spend their lifetime trying to drown out the messages that were recorded in their brains early in life.

Incidentally, I was thrilled to learn years later that Billy William Racecar received a tennis scholarship from the University of Southern California. I didn't hear anything about Pedro.

Managing the Shame Pile

You may be tempted about now to say, "There, you see, Marilyn? Little Racecar made it in life. All you shrink types who constantly harp about the harm we do to our children give me fits. So Billy William didn't ever feel like 'the best'—it sure didn't seem to ruin him. He rose above it all. And rising above the negative is a necessity for living life! No one has a perfect background with perfect smiling parents who know exactly how and when to discipline and just exactly how to make their child know the discipline was about his behavior and not his person."

And you're absolutely right! No one on the face of the earth parents perfectly. Every single one of us can remember at least a bazillion times (I sure can) when we have blown it as parents. And yes, we all have to learn how to rise above the negative input we've received as kids and continue to receive even as adults. But here's the point: The fact that we rise above the negativity and are outward successes is not the issue. The issue is that all that hurtful, shame-producing stuff is not eliminated simply because we've managed to excel. The shame pile still exists, giving rise to self-talk that continually causes us to question our core value. As long as that shame-inspired self-talk goes on, we will work harder and harder to prove the internal messages wrong.

One of the many possible patterns that the shame mind-set can produce is workaholism: "Enough is never enough" is the thinking behind that pattern. No matter how hard the workaholic person performs or how successfully the goals are reached, he or she still has the sense that it could have been better.

The "enough-is-never-enough" shame voice also affects relationships. This person has trouble receiving love because she believes that somehow love, like everything else in life, has to be earned; she has to qualify. Simply hearing the words "I love you" sets off myriad internal responses, such as, "You wouldn't say that if you really knew me." "Once you know me you won't love me because I'm not as good or successful as I may appear." "It'd be safer for me to keep you at a distance so that you don't find out the truth about me." "I guess I'll marry you, but you'll never get very close to me because I've got to work very hard so you'll continue to think you love me because love is based upon what I do and not who I am. Besides, I have to work very hard just to feel good about myself, so no matter how you look at it, my first priority, my basic commitment, will be to my work. It's doing well in life that assures me I'm valuable."

Let me give you one more example of how shame can take up lodging at a very early age due to, in this case, unwise mothering. (Before you drop the book and dash off to pour yourself a little cup of strychnine, this is the last example. I promise we'll conclude this chapter on a more upbeat note!)

My father was born into what he described as "a litter" of ten children. From his earliest memory he felt like an unwanted burden: yet another mouth to feed, another body to clothe and house. Repeatedly his mother told not only him, but all the children, that she wished they had never been born. It was her custom that whoever was closest at hand, she'd reach out and smack him or her on whatever part of the body was nearest, saying, "That slap was for whatever you shouldn't have done that I missed." It never occurred to her to make up for the hugs they all missed.

Many shame messages were etched into my father's psyche as he grew up, but one of the more pronounced was his shame for having needs. Since his and the other children's basic needs for food, shelter, and clothing seemed most to upset his mother, Dad, without being able to label it as such, felt he shouldn't have those needs and was ashamed that he did.

He determined very early in his life that as soon as he possibly could, he would leave home and tend to his own needs so as to no longer be a burden. At the age of thirteen, he did indeed leave home, vowing never to return. Out of respect for the poverty of his family, he sent a portion of his hard-earned wages as a sawmill worker to his mother each month. Slowly he earned enough money to leave eastern Canada and go to the United States, where he ultimately put himself through school and became a pastor.

Later, as Dad looked back on his childhood, he understood his mother a little better. She had ten children by the time she was thirty-five. Her husband, who was a tender man but in poor health, was able to provide very little for the family. Responsibility for everyone's well-being rested upon this young mother's tired and overworked shoulders. They barely survived. Dad felt regret for her hard life but felt no love for his mom. He had no desire to ever see her again, especially since his kindly father had died.

I well remember meeting this grandmother for the first time when I was fourteen. She was determined to make the long trip from eastern Canada to Washington State because Jasper (my father) was the only son who'd never come home. She had not seen him in thirty-one years.

My grandmother was a little fireball of a woman with eyes so blue they were nearly black; they literally sparkled with intensity and humor. I shared my bedroom with her and we laughed and giggled late into the night during her five-day visit. One day she tried to teach me how to make an apron. When I sewed the pocket in upside down (which kept it perpetually empty), my grandmother laughed so hard she simply collapsed on the floor. I loved her.

The day she left she attempted to give my father some money. He politely but coldly refused it, saying, "I have no needs, Mother." Her response was, "Please take it; it's for all the times I missed." He again refused it and, with a formal handshake, put her on the train.

As we drove away from the train station, my mother turned to Dad and quietly said, "Why, Jasper, it would have meant so much to her for you to take the money." His curt response was simply, "It's too late."

I was utterly mystified by the behavior of my normally warm, fun-loving father. In fact, I hadn't been able to figure out why he had treated his mother with such cold courtesy all week. She was wonderfully fun, loving, and great to be with as far as I was concerned. I had also noted that my mother was extremely kind and solicitous toward her. What in the world was wrong with my father?

Now, years later, I know what was wrong with my father, and the knowledge breaks my heart. All Dad knew as a little fellow was that he was unwanted and a burden. In addition, he was mistreated. It never occurred to him that he was in reality a gifted, delightful child who was lovable and capable of being a joy to any mother. Neither did it occur to him that this inherently warm and fun-loving mother was so desperately overwhelmed as well as unschooled in parenting skills that she was unable to cope. No child understands that kind of complexity. The only message that was seared into Dad's psyche with the intensity of a branding iron was that he was a person unworthy of even the food, shelter, and clothing he so desperately needed to survive. Unable to fend for himself regarding those basic needs, Dad assumed there was something wrong with needing—something wrong with him, not with his mother and not with their circumstances. In his mind, he was nothing more than an inconvenience and a burden. Shame took up residence in Dad's heart and never left.

The result was that Dad never reconciled with his mother and never forgave her for her inability to parent under crushingly adverse circumstances. In his mind he understood, but in his heart he remained unmoved. He hung on to his fierce independence and determination to need nothing from anyone until the day he died.

I so wish Dad had understood the insidiousness of the shame that prevented him from experiencing healing release, the freedom to forgive, and the God-given right to appreciate his true value. Even though he was an effective minister and sincere communicator of the gospel of grace, there was that one dark corner of his heart's left side that grace did not penetrate or heal. Why? He didn't understand shame's crippling effects upon his life. He understood salvation and how it was attained through a relationship with Jesus Christ. He understood prayer and his need of spiritual communion. But he never understood or addressed the fact that he was housing a colossal lie that hissed out demeaning messages about his worth. He attempted to drown out the messages by working harder, hoping to minister more and more effectively in the lives of others.

Tragically, I'm afraid that is true for so many of us. The shame that insists we have no value runs totally contrary to the Bible's message that says we are of such value we are worth the death of God's only Son on the cross. Over and over again in Scripture God declares His unfailing love and His unconditional caring for His creation, and yet that message more often than not falls on shame-deafened ears. In spite of the preaching of grace, shame is still an imperious presence in many of our hearts and our churches today.

The good news is there is a cure for imperfection that leads to shame, which causes us to live in denial and fear. You'll be glad to know that the cure is not a pill, and you'll never be wrestled to the floor to take it!

Chat Room Possibilities

1. Discuss a time when you couldn't seem to admit to being wrong.

2. What are some of the elaborate cover-ups you use to divert recognition that you are less than perfect?

3. Can you pinpoint the first time you experienced shame?

4. Was your childhood home one in which you felt valued and affirmed? If so, what specifically did your parents do to make you feel valued?

5. Examine some of your behavioral patterns and determine if any of them springs from a shame base. Is it possible to change the behavior? How?

6

Shame in the Church?

SPREADING GOD'S
GRACE TO THE HURTING

I am experiencing what I fear is an age-related malady that is becoming increasingly and alarmingly apparent in me. My speech is nearly devoid of nouns; all too often persons, places, and things totally elude me as I'm attempting to carry on a conversation. I'll give you an example.

"Sheila, I had the most enjoyable lunch today with . . . um . . . I had lunch with . . . oh, you know . . . that woman whose husband invested in hamsters last year . . ."

"Hamsters, Marilyn? I don't know anyone who invested in hamsters last year. Why in the world would anyone invest in hamsters?"

"I don't know . . . I think he thought they'd be the ideal pet for the new millennium . . . they're low maintenance, take up little space, etc. I guess he assumed he could make some quick money. But that's not the point."

"Okay, Marilyn, maybe you'd remember the point and the name of the lady you had lunch with if you told me where you ate."

"We ate at a fabulous Mexican restaurant called . . . um . . . you know . . . the one with the fountain in the middle of the patio and if you sit too close to it your shoes get wet . . . you know, the one I mean . . . it's near that specialty shop that sells uh . . ."

I'll spare you further illustration, but the knowledge that I am becoming conversationally tedious is hard on my ego, especially since my eyesight is still good and I can see people quietly slipping out of the room.

The most difficult element of my condition is not just the tediousness of my lapses, but I'm starting to remind myself of Mrs. Tubular. She was without a doubt the most horrific Sunday-school teacher God ever called into children's ministry. (Actually, God didn't call her. I don't know where her call came from, but I have a guess.) She too had a noun deficit. Typically she would start a Bible story by saying, "There once was a tiny little man named, um . . . uh . . ." Someone would shout out, "Zaccheus!" Moving ahead, ". . . and because he was short and wanted to see Jesus when Jesus came through, um . . . um . . ." "Jericho!" the same smart kid would mercifully shout. The entire story hour was spent in those kinds of student rescue missions. Now, in view of my current state, I can muster some empathy for my Sunday-school teacher, but at that stage in my life I prayed for the return of Christ.

However, the problem with Mrs. Tubular was far more serious than her inability to seize her elusive nouns. The problem was she had me frightfully convinced that I was not a Christian, that I was in fact a sinner beyond hope whose future would be spent burning in hell!

These dire predictions were frequently given to all of us eight-year-old pagans. It was her method of control. Whenever one of us would "get out of line," she'd stop her story narrative and launch into a description of hell that would make Dante's *Inferno* look compelling in comparison.

I falteringly told her one Sunday that I had become a Christian when I was five years old and that my mother told me Christians went to heaven when they died, not hell. She shot back a scathing response saying that I was only "playacting" when I asked Jesus into my heart because if I really had become a Christian I wouldn't be such a bad girl. (My badness consisted of talking too much and getting the giggles over her consistent inability to complete a sentence.)

But the message that really slathered the shame all over me was when she told me I must be an embarrassment to my parents. "After all," she said, "your daddy is the pastor of this church, and he must be so ashamed that his very own daughter is always bad and even lies by saying she's a Christian."

I hated the thought that I was so bad hell was waiting for me, but I also hated the idea of being an embarrassment to my parents. They were very nice people. They didn't deserve such a rotten kid.

Oddly enough, I never told my parents about Mrs. Tubular's hair-raising description of hell or her low opinion of her pastor's only child. Instead, I tried hard to improve my behavior. I mentally practiced my multiplication tables in an attempt to distract myself from Mrs. Tubular's storytelling style and made every effort, which included feigning laryngitis, to speak to no one.

Fortunately, one of the parents in the church went to my father and complained about Mrs. Tubular. (It was the mother of the boy who diligently filled in her noun blanks.) My father was horrified that all the little eight-year-olds in her class, including his daughter, were convinced they were bound for hell because they were so bad. Mrs. Tubular was immediately removed from her teaching position and put in charge of the monthly church suppers. In that role she couldn't do anything more harmful than burn the meat loaf.

My parents then assured me that not only was my conversion experience real when it occurred at the age of five, but that no one is headed for hell just because he or she is naughty. Hell is a place for those who have never received Jesus as Savior. Confessing our sin is what we're to do when we're naughty; we need not pack our flame-retardant pajamas and wait on the corner for the Hades Express.

My parents were also quick to assure me that I was not an embarrassment to them and that just because my dad was the pastor didn't mean I had to sport a halo and squelch all my childish instincts in an effort to be a good example. They did, however, point out that my tendency to talk and giggle came up on my report cards with a fair amount of consistency. We all agreed it would be wise to make an effort to curb that behavior. (I'm still working on that.)

Spiritual Abuse

With the exception of Mrs. Tubular, I was fortunate to have no more spiritually shaming experiences as I grew up. (Her harrowing descriptions of hell stayed with me for years, though.) To my surprise and dismay, however, the kind of abuse she inflicted is apparently not all that uncommon. During my days as a therapist I would usually ask my clients about their spiritual persuasions. Although I was known as a Christian counselor, many of my clients were unbelievers. It was troublesome to learn of the many abuses some of them had experienced in the church. The result for many was a rejection of any kind of faith system at all.

One especially disturbing, shaming experience was told to me by an extremely bitter man named David who was in his late forties. As a teenager he had sex with one of the girls in his church group. The first sexual experience for either of them, it resulted in a pregnancy. Terrified of the consequences, the boy paid for an abortion. He and his girlfriend swore to keep it a secret between them.

With the passing of time, however, the girl went into a depression that startled and mystified her parents. She ate very little and lost interest in her studies and all school activities. The only thing she wanted to do was sleep. Ultimately she broke down and told her parents what had happened.

Stunned by their seemingly perfect daughter's confession, they told her she had not only shamed herself and her family, but she had shamed the name of Christ as well. Then they confronted the boy and his family. Since both families went to the same church, they called their pastor and met him in his church office.

Just prior to the Sunday morning sermon, the pastor asked the two families to come and stand before the congregation. They were instructed to then make a public confession of their individual sins. The boy and girl confessed to their fornication, lying, and murder of their baby. The parents confessed to their sin of ineffective parenting, which resulted in the shameful behavior of their children. The pastor admonished both young people to consider the condition of their hearts and recognize that based on their behavior, it was clear that neither had ever actually received Christ as Savior. At the conclusion of the service no one in the congregation spoke to the members of either family.

My client never returned to that church (just more evidence of his sin-hardened heart, according to the pastor). David assumed that if the church found him so shameful, God must see him the same way. There was no point then in ever going to church and certainly no point in praying to a God who was utterly appalled by him and probably wouldn't hear him anyway.

We talked at great length in one of our sessions about the contrast between his pastor's lack of compassion and the compassion of Jesus toward the woman caught in adultery, recorded in John 8. The Pharisees were attempting to publicly shame her as well as put Jesus on the spot to see if He would sanction the Mosaic Law of stoning her to death for her sin. When instead Jesus said, "Let him who is without sin among you be the first to throw a stone at her," he forced the accusers to face their own inherently sinful state. Each one gradually slunk away, leaving only Jesus and the humiliated woman. He didn't make her stand in the temple and confess to everyone her wrongdoing. He instead preserved her shredded dignity and told her to go and sin no more.

My friend David's dignity had been destroyed when he was a young man, and in that context there was no gentle but firm divine encouragement to go and sin no more. He was instead ostracized and made to feel like, in his words, "vermin."

He never fully recovered although he ultimately married, had three daughters, and built a very successful career. On the surface, no one would guess his inner sense of worthlessness and shame. No one, that is, but the God who never ceased to love him and who longed to receive his confession and restore him to the assurance of his salvation and priceless value.

Paul Tournier, the highly respected Christian Swiss psychiatrist, wrote, "The Church proclaims the grace of God. And moralism, which is the negation of it, always creeps back into its bosom. . . . Grace becomes conditional. Judgment appears. . . . I see every day its ravages in . . . all the Christian Churches."[1]

Brennan Manning writes in *Ruthless Trust* about a youth worker at a church in a midwestern town who dared to confess to the staff one morning that he struggled with pornography. He received his letter of termination that afternoon.

Throwing Stones

One of the most chilling accounts of abuse I've ever read is a secular short story entitled "The Lottery," by Shirley Jackson. I taught it a number of times during my tenure at Biola University. At the beginning of the story we are charmed by the gentle sweetness of a little village where "the flowers were blossoming profusely and the grass was richly green." We listen in on the folksy verbal exchanges between the various persons gathering together in the village square for some kind of annual traditional event that everyone hopes would conclude in time for lunch.

We see Mrs. Hutchinson come hurriedly along the path to the square, her sweater thrown over her shoulders as she breathlessly glides into place beside her husband. Drying her hands on her apron she says, "Clean forgot what day it was and then I looked out the window and the kids were gone and then I remembered it was the 27th and I came a runnin." Everyone good-naturedly assures her she has arrived on time and that the proceedings are just beginning.

Mr. Summers, the town official, then instructs each person to come forward, select a small slip of paper from the centuries-old black box, and keep it folded.

"After that there was a long pause, a breathless pause until Mr. Summers holding his slip of paper in the air, said, 'All right folks.' For a minute no one moved, and then all the slips of paper were opened. 'Who is it?' 'Who's got it?'"

There is a general sigh throughout the crowd as people individually held up their papers so all could see they were blank. But when Mr. Summers read Tessie Hutchinson's name so she could show her paper, it had to be forced out of her hand. It had the black mark on it. Her husband Bill held it up "and there was a stir in the crowd."

The pile of stones the boys had made earlier was ready; there were stones on the ground with the blowing scraps of paper that had come out of the box. Mrs. Delacroix [Tessie's friend and neighbor] selected a stone so large she had to pick it up with both hands. She turned to Mrs. Dunbar. "Come on," she said. "Hurry up!"

Mrs. Dunbar had small stones in both hands, and she said, gasping for breath, "I can't run at all. You'll have to go ahead and I'll catch up with you."

The children had stones all ready, and someone gave little Davey Hutchinson a few pebbles. Tessie Hutchinson was in the center of a cleared space by now, and she held her hands out desperately as the villagers moved in on her. "It isn't fair," she said. A stone hit her on the side of the head. "It isn't fair, it isn't right." Mrs. Hutchinson screamed and then they were upon her.

Horrifying as this story of human sacrifice is, I wonder if at times we don't gather up our pile of stones in the name of church discipline, righteous indignation, or fidelity to the truth and search out the persons with black marks. The persons who have divorced or struggled with homosexuality, adultery, alcohol, drugs, or pornography may all too often find themselves in the "cleared space," frightened and ashamed as we begin to hurl our stones.

Of course these stones don't look like stones; in fact, they have no shape at all. But they can be felt and they can be heard. These are the stones of criticism, rejection, abandonment, shunning, and exclusion. Perhaps the loudest stone is "You don't fit here and, because of your behavior, you're not welcome here." Deeply ashamed, the person escapes the cleared space and disappears, sometimes forever.

I asked my students what they thought Jesus would do if He were to come upon the villagers on the verge of stoning Mrs. Hutchinson. They all thought He'd put a stop to the proceedings immediately. One girl in the class went so far as to say she could just see Jesus holding up His hand and commanding that the villagers drop their rocks. Then He would walk over to Mrs. Hutchinson, lift her to her feet, and say, "I am come that you might have life."

I'd like to further suggest that Jesus would then explain that everyone, not just Mrs. Hutchinson, has a black mark and that He died for all the black marks in the world. No one ever has to die because of a black mark. "As a result, he [Jesus] has brought you into the very presence of God, and you are holy and blameless as you stand before him without a single fault" (Col. 1:22 NLT). What a great ending for that story!

It seems to me that we in the Christian community need to look for a better ending to the stories that touch our lives every day. If we ceased to shame our members and instead came alongside in love and

SHAME IN THE CHURCH?

support, we could be instruments of grace. Because Jesus, who never has a noun deficit, calls us each by name and says, "I have chosen you and will not throw you away" (Isa. 41:9 NLT).

The Shame Cure

Every Christian should know this fundamental truth and behave accordingly: The only antidote for shame is grace! As Martin Luther wrote, "No one can be good and do good unless God's grace first makes him good; and no one becomes good by works, but good works are done only by Him who is good." But for the shame-shackled person in a church where performance and good works are overemphasized, the shame persists and even becomes more deeply rooted. How tragic! As psychiatrist Paul Tournier suggests happens in so many churches, grace becomes conditional. We sing the shame-producing words "I gave, I gave My life for thee, what hast thou given to Me?" failing to realize that hymn is not a call to works, but to salvation. It is a plea to give one's heart and soul to the One who died for that heart and soul. It is not a mandate to rush out and try to "pay God back" in order to be worthy of what He gave freely.

Similarly, we hear Matthew 5:48 preached, in which Jesus said, "You, therefore, must be perfect, as your heavenly Father is perfect." The shame-shackled person rises up with clattering chains and makes a pitiful effort then to be as perfect as Jesus. We'll be miserably clattering about the rest of our lives if we think our efforts and good works will make us perfect! And as long as some churches preach that we must be perfect, we'll once again miss grace and instead embrace human effort, the inevitable failure of which leads back to the dead end of shame.

Romans 3 states emphatically, "We are utterly incapable of living the glorious lives God wills for us. God did it for us. Out of sheer generosity he put us in right standing with himself. A pure gift. He got us out of the mess we're in and restored us to where he always wanted us to be. And he did it by means of Jesus Christ. God sacrificed Jesus on the altar of the world to clear that world of sin. Having faith in him sets us in the clear" (MSG). How are we made perfect like Jesus? Only through the indwelling presence of the perfect One. Faith in Him alone "sets us in the clear," free of the need to perform to earn what He's already given us. Mind-boggling!

In his excellent book *The Grace Awakening*, Chuck Swindoll writes, "When the grace of Christ is fully awake in your life, you find you're no longer doing something due to fear or out of shame or because of guilt, but you're doing it through love. The dreadful tyranny of performing in order to please someone is over . . . forever."[2] That's the liberating message of the gospel of Jesus Christ.

Shame is recognizable because it communicates to us that we are nothing more than a walking, talking mistake. If that's how we feel about ourselves, then we've got digging to do. The average apology for the shame-based person is, "Excuse me for living." Does anyone deserve to feel that way? Absolutely not! When we understand that those shame messages are not deserved—that they are, in fact, lies—we can grab the biggest shovel we can find and start digging, rooting out, and discarding. Yahoo!

God sent His Son, Jesus, to be for us what we could never be: perfect. As a result, in the eyes of God the Father we have priceless value! Shame has no right to lodge within us or dictate who we are. Messages that undermine, criticize, and demean have no basis in fact. The fact is that we are children of the King! I know that; perhaps you know that. Why, then, does shame still sometimes cripple us and rob us of peace?

We know and we don't know. We know that a wonderful transformation occurs within us when the Son of God enters our lives, assuring us of salvation, forgiveness of sin, and ultimate hope of eternity in the presence of our all-loving Creator. And yet we often fail to recognize that shame, which is not sin, still lurks about in the corners of our hearts in spite of the infilling of the Spirit of God. It is shame that keeps us from knowing God's fullness of joy. It is shame that the enemy uses against us to keep us hobbled, uncertain, and at times ineffective in relationships. It is shame that inspires the freneticism of having to do more and be more.

So what do we do about this lingering shame? To begin, I think we have to know what kind of shame we're dealing with; we need to literally see the face of the enemy. Where did that shame come from, and how and when did it get there? If, for example, my dad had had the benefit of living in a more psychologically aware era, perhaps someone could have helped him identify, face, and understand those deep-seated, shame-based lies that took root in his soul at such an early age. Once he faced his internal enemy (which was *not* his own human need), he could have gone to battle against it. He hopefully could have come to a place of compassion for his mother and realized that though her statements were the source of his shame, those statements were both untrue and undeserved. Once knowing that, he could then ask for what he needed most, which was to invite the healing presence of Jesus to evict those shame-hissing lodgers off the property of his heart's left side. He could have claimed at a heart level what he knew to be scripturally true: "By entering through faith into what God has always wanted to do for us—set us right with him, make us fit for him—we have it all together with God because of our Master Jesus" (Rom. 5:1 MSG).

God through Jesus has made us "fit for him"—perfect! If shame messages creep back into our minds, we need only to claim again that we are once and for all "set . . . right with him." That is an absolute, undeniable, divine truth. If feelings, which have no brains, try to interfere with that truth for us, we must claim it again and again for ourselves. We cannot allow the brainless to distract us or to lead us away from what God has declared to be a fact.

In conclusion, all the knowledge of the origin of our shame, the reason for our shame, or the perpetrator of our shame will not ulti-mately heal us. God alone is the healer. Our part is to bring that spe-cific, now named and recognized shame to Him. Because lies crouch in darkness, the penetrating light of God will cast out those lies that seek to keep us from luxuriating in the simple truth that we are indeed the apple of His eye, in spite of whatever we've heard and learned to believe about ourselves.

Moving toward Abundance

For the sake of quick review, I want to say again that we do not actu-ally, literally, have divided hearts; we don't really have split sides. Our "stuff"—the good and the bad—cohabitate with, at times, a shaky truce. I use the image of the zipper down the middle of the heart dividing the bad and the good in an effort to help us see that we all, absolutely all, have parts of us we'd prefer to hide. My thinking is that perhaps by en-visioning our hearts as "zippered," we can more clearly see what is going on in us. Hopefully we can recognize that what so many of us do is kick the stuff we don't like into the heart's left side, all the while denying we kicked anything anywhere. We present our heart's right side to the pub-lic, family, friends, and, whenever possible, to ourselves and even to God. We present the right side because it reflects us as we want to appear.

The problem with that method is the nagging knowledge that we really aren't as good as we try to appear, which creates all kinds of inner disquiet. The crabby little inner voice clicks on and accuses us of being a fake . . . a hypocrite . . . maybe not even a Christian. The result-ing shame impels us to outfit ourselves with a variety of masks in an almost desperate effort to look like we think we should look. All the while, we're afraid we aren't anywhere near the quality person we think we ought to be, others think we are, or worse yet, God says we should be!

How comforting to remember that God sees both sides of us at once and, because of the cross, sees us as perfect as Jesus is perfect. But many of us miss that crucial truth and give in to the pressure to be better and look better. As a result, we employ the tried-and-true method of denial. And, as you'll recall, the problem with denial is it keeps us in denial! (Sometimes I am so profound I can hardly stand it.) And what causes us to grab denial and clutch it like a down comforter in zero-degree weather? Shame. Shame that we aren't better, can't seem to get better, and don't deserve to be better anyway!

So for goodness' sake, we think, *let's not look into the denied shame stuff because we don't want to feel it and don't even want to look at it!* Some of us think such ignorance is bliss. The enemy would love to have us think so. Why? Because as long as we're a little, or even a lot, ashamed of ourselves, we'll never know God's peace that passes understanding. Shame keeps us ashamed! (You can quote me on that.)

The enemy is totally invested in keeping God's people in a perceived state of unworthiness and shame. If he can keep us there, we won't ever really know what the abundant life Jesus invited us to in John 10:10 is all about. We'll even think the abundant life isn't possible and that perhaps Jesus was exaggerating the offer just a bit. (That's one of the enemy's favorite tactics: to discredit the promises of God or, if we don't buy into that, convince us that His promises are experienced by everyone else except us.)

Here's the bottom-line truth I keep having to remind myself of: At the moment of conversion to Christ, Satan lost the battle for my eternal soul. But he'll never stop the daily war he wages against my spiritual well-being, my peace, my security, and the sure knowledge that I am loved beyond measure by my heavenly Father in spite of the shame that sometimes drapes itself around my inner being. God intends for me to be free of shame and to discard the denial habit. But to do so, not only do I need to believe He truly does mean for me to experience daily peace, security, and the assurance of His limitless love, but I also need to carefully examine the pileup in my heart's left side so I'll know specifically what is keeping me buried in shame and exempt from abundance.

In the next chapter we'll scrutinize another familiar and toxic tenant: guilt.

Chat Room Possibilities

1. Have you ever had a spiritually shaming experience that drove you from the church?

2. Do you agree or disagree with Paul Tournier's statement: "The Church proclaims the grace of God. And moralism [legalism] . . . always creeps back into its bosom"?

3. To what degree is grace conditional in your thinking? In other words, do you think, *Grace is real, grace is great, but I must earn it somehow by doing good things. Otherwise, I don't deserve it.*

4. What did Martin Luther mean in the following quote: "No one can be good and do good unless God's grace first makes him good; and no one becomes good by works, but good works are done only by Him who is good"?

5. Have you ever been the target of "stone throwers"? Have you ever been a stone thrower yourself?

A Tall Tale

GETTING A GRIP
ON OUR GUILT

In 1966, the British Broadcasting Company ran a spoof on one of their nightly TV news programs. It was a five-minute documentary on the complexities of spaghetti-growing in Italy. Without the slightest hint of humor, the announcer told the audience that throughout Italy millions of pasta farmers were working harder than ever before to harvest their pasta before it fell prey to the pests that ravaged much of last season's crop. Footage showed farmers in broad-brimmed hats working their way up neatly trimmed aisles of spaghetti trees in the Italian farmlands. The viewers watched the farmers plucking sun-ripened strands of spaghetti from the branches and storing them in wicker baskets. The announcer concluded the coverage by saying that special efforts had been taken that year to ward off the spaghetti wee-vil, which had been especially destructive in recent years. This report was made to the BBC viewers with no reference to satire or levity. Apparently millions of them did not question the fact that spaghetti grows on trees.

As improbable as it might seem that people would swallow that tall tale, some of us swallow equally tall tales about ourselves. We believe that if we don't look attractive, seem intelligent, smell good, and have matching clothes, we ought to stay in the house. We believe that as long as we're doing relatively well in our jobs, with our kids, with our spouses, and with our yards, we have value. We also believe that if we make mistakes, the yard turns brown, the kids are arrested, we wear green shoes with a navy suit, and we're fired from the job, we have no value . . . no worth . . . we should be shot!

Probably we feel guilty: If the truth were known, it's our fault the rain won't let up; somehow everything that's wrong in life can be traced to something we're doing wrong. Now that's another tall tale! But I know plenty of people who swallow that tale. On occasion, I'm one of them.

We all feel guilty from time to time, and guilt is not always a bad thing. It can, in fact, be a very good thing. Guilt is a valuable restraint for a society that might be tempted to run red lights, sleep with the neighbor, or shoplift at Macy's. Guilt can keep us from yelling at the kids or kicking the dog. When guilt restrains people from unrighteous behavior, it benefits civilization and assures us of a well-ordered world. It's as if we cart around a little blue-suited police officer who either holds up her hand or waves us on.

Now that may sound like conscience, but conscience is not the same as guilt. Guilt springs from something we've done that we don't approve of. Conscience assures us that we were right in disapproving. Conscience is, in essence, the ability to know right and wrong. Guilt is what we feel when conscience is ignored and wrongdoing occurs anyway. Guilt is connected to behavior. We might behave in an unattractive manner and as a result feel guilty. We relieve that guilt by apologizing or rectifying the situation in some way.

When I was teaching at Biola University, a young man in my American literature class was struggling in every way possible. His writing skills were underdeveloped, his ability to critique novels was lacking, and he saw no reason to acquire these skills. One of the class assignments was to write a paper on the moral implications of the novel *Ethan Frome*. That sent him over the edge. Unbeknownst to me, he hired his girlfriend to write the paper. For payment, he agreed to take her to six L.A. Lakers' basketball games. (His dad had seats on the floor, a few feet from the players' chairs.)

He turned in a fantastic paper that received a resounding A grade. I must admit that I was a bit surprised at his well-expressed insights, but after all, I thought humbly, perhaps my fine teaching sparked a flicker of genius in his yet unignited literary passion. Not so.

After suffering a lot of inner turmoil, he confessed to me his A was undeserved, that he had not written the paper, and that the only thing he could say about the character Ethan Frome was that he was a wimp! That one thought could not produce a paper, he realized sadly, and as far as he knew, the idea had no kinship to moral commentary.

As he left my office, I asked him if he would still take his girlfriend to the Lakers' games. Grinning, he told me he would because he couldn't bear the moral implications if he didn't. I liked that kid, even though I had to give him an F on his paper, which resulted in a D for the course. He at least had the courage to confess to me and make it right.

Another example of appropriate guilt is what a workaholic husband and father experienced. His boys were born and grew up barely knowing their father because he was seldom home. His wife, who immersed herself in innumerable school and civic activities, became so used to his absence she rarely thought to include him in the family's plans. He realized too late the price he paid for his professional and financial success. His guilt and regret propelled him to attempt to make up for the lost time. His adult sons were thrilled to have access to their dad and graciously received his tearful apologies for his parental neglect. His wife was also delighted to "have him back" and remembered then why she had been attracted to him in the first place. This is a guilt story with a happy ending.

There are times when we need to feel guilty about what we do and other times when our guilt comes from swallowing a tall tale that says we can't make mistakes . . . ever. This kind of guilt comes from our desire to be without flaws. We learn early in life that mistakes and wrong behavior are not rewarded. Our parents aren't happy when misbehavior occurs; depending on the severity of the parent and the sensitivity of the child, mistakes can be totally unacceptable. If the child makes a mistake, she faces the risk that approval, acceptance, and love (the most powerful and sought-after commodity by all human beings) will be withdrawn. These are devastating fears for the child. If love is withdrawn, then the fear of abandonment and isolation becomes an overwhelming threat.

To avoid these consequences, the child learns early that the world can be a good place as long as she doesn't mess up. If she messes up, she feels guilty because messes are unacceptable. Messes mean she's a mess . . . if she's a mess, love is withdrawn . . . and on and on the cycle goes. The tragedy is that many of us don't outgrow the cycle. It plays itself out in the adult who can't ever be wrong. Being right protects the fragile self from guilt and all its emotional repercussions.

At this point we need to revisit the subject of shame because shame and guilt work in partnership, and it's helpful to understand that partnership. Unhealthy shame comes developmentally before guilt. The budding little psyche first experiences shame as an infant who is a mass of sensory perceptions for which there are yet no words. If the infant is handled roughly, if the voices are harsh and the infant's need to be cuddled, held, and rocked is basically ignored, the infant develops shame. Of course that is not a verbalization. It is a powerful sense communicated to the infant's psyche. Were the infant able to verbalize that sense, she would say simply, "I am unlovable."

Depending on the type of neglect, there are varying levels of shame, all of which develop during infancy and then may be built upon as the child develops. Children who in their first three years have experienced abuse, deprivation, or abandonment have psyches so damaged and swaddled in shame, they frequently are unable to function normally.

Remember, shame differs from guilt in that shame springs not from a behavior, but from a state of being. Shame dictates how we see ourselves. If we say, "I am worthless, inferior, and without redeeming qualities; I don't deserve anything good because I am so bad," then we're talking from beneath a huge compost pile of shame. Guilt then hooks up with that shame and says, "I abuse alcohol and drugs because I can't bear to see how bad I am. Substances keep me from seeing and feeling who I fear I am." The substance abuse is the behavior; shame is the feeding tube. Guilt is about what we do; shame is about who we think we are.

Now perhaps you, like I, did not experience great deprivation as an infant. Though you recognize the unhealthy shame messages that seep up from the floor of your soul from time to time, you are functioning quite well. Yes, there are times when guilt grips your being like a size-two leotard, but still, you are functioning quite well.

In spite of our seemingly healthy functioning, I'd like to point out some patterns of behavior that really are not healthy, even though they may not be recognizable to others and possibly to our selves. To discuss these patterns, I'm going to use myself as an example in an effort to illustrate that sometimes guilt and shame can work together in subtle but unhealthy ways.

To begin with, I overcommit by taking on more projects than I have time for. If I have the opportunity to do something that has merit and might make the world a better place, I have to be in on it. The justification for my committing to these projects is that they're good projects. "Well, good grief, Marilyn," you say, "so you're a tad busy. How do you drag guilt and shame in on that?" I'll tell you.

I grew up in a family in which service to others was highly valued. My pastor father was hardworking and had no other staff persons at church. Among other things, he regularly called on his parishioners, prepared his sermons, married and buried, made himself fully available to the community, and fell into bed each night exhausted. In addition to other tasks, my mother taught school, typed and printed the church bulletin, directed the choir, and taught a Sunday-school class. She too fell into bed exhausted each night. Their lives were an inspiration to me; my memories of their dedicated ministry are sweet.

I was unaware of their exhaustion at the time. I was never told that I had to "go and do likewise," neither did I feel overt pressure from them to live up to their standard of service. Nonetheless, I have put pressure on myself to be a tribute to them—a source of pleasure, perhaps even pride. If I did not produce, if I took the easy route in any endeavor, the crabby little voice in my ear would say, *You're a bit of a sloth, Marilyn . . . Your parents certainly weren't . . . Where did that lazy streak come from?* These are shame messages because they came as a result of my thoughts and emotions, not my behavior.

There was another pressure to produce, the significance of which I've only recently grasped. It springs from what I call the only-child syndrome. Since I was the only kid who could bring potential pleasure and reward to my parents, I worked hard to do just that. I didn't want them to feel cheated because they hadn't had other children. When I was awarded "most outstanding girl" graduate of my high-school class, that award felt almost like payment to my parents. They would be stunned to know I carried these thoughts and feelings, but I did. I put pressure on myself to do all and be all that a larger family might have been for my parents.

I also realize I've worked to accomplish goals my father's circumstances prevented him from accomplishing. He loved education and longed deeply to have more. I think the reason I acquired two master's degrees is that he would have loved that for himself. Somehow by obtaining the education my father never had, I've attempted to fulfill his longings.

How does guilt figure into the shame-based way of operating? Very simply. When I'm not accomplishing, producing, or contributing, I feel guilty. Neither of my parents would want that for me, but the feeling is there nonetheless. I have to be careful and monitor how much I do and determine for whom I'm doing it. Is it really for God, or is it to assure my parents that it was a good thing I was born?

As a result of this kind of thinking and believing, I can all too often be described as more of a human *doing* than a human *being*. As my children were growing up, I was so busy doing good things that I sometimes missed *their* good things. Why? I had a legacy to live up to, and I would be ashamed not to reflect well on that legacy. I recognize now that my preoccupation with performing well sometimes came at the expense of those I love dearly.

The second guilt pattern I'd like to discuss is hating to be wrong. Earlier we discussed how being wrong opens up the guilt-prone person to the threat of being inferior . . . defective. "If I'm defective, you'll think less of me . . . remove your love from me. If I'm wrong, you will not only remove your love from me, you might not respect me, which means you probably won't want to go out to lunch with me anymore!" Mercy! That's serious.

Oddly enough, I don't mind admitting that I'm wrong; I just hate the fact of being wrong. (Just to make sure I'm not in denial here I asked some friends whose honesty I trust if they thought I admitted to being wrong easily. They assured me I did not mind saying, "I'm wrong." Apparently because of much practice with the phrase, I say it convincingly.)

My resistance to being wrong can be over something as stupid as the closure of Cook Street by my house. It seems as if every time I set out on my mundane errands, a nearby street is torn up with yellow-helmeted men scurrying around in the holes they've dug. Cook Street has been either torn up or closed for days, but yesterday I forgot that when I left the house at 8 A.M. In spite of following the detours, knocking over five cones, and slowing to a crawl because I was reduced to one lane, I arrived at the grocery store before sundown. By then, I'd forgotten why I came! I berated myself all the way home with shame messages such as, *Marilyn, it really isn't all that hard to remember street closures . . . just think . . . just remember. But then I suppose you're really not all that bright now, are you?*

I may never recover from the guilt and shame I feel about my silicone implant experience. That whole thing was wrong! What I was told would be a nonthreatening enhancement to my body has turned out to be anything but that. I've lost nearly a year of productivity to the effects of silicone toxicity (producing guilt over what I'm not accomplishing) and may have health challenges yet to face with that poison wandering around my body (producing more guilt because I've put my health in jeopardy). In addition is the crabby shame voice that says, *Why couldn't you have been content with the body God gave you? So what if you're the only woman you know who doesn't need a bra?* (Now there's a shame voice if ever there was one . . . Dragging God into it makes me really feel ashamed!)

Amid these already clamoring shame messages is the clincher, which clamors the loudest: *What will other people think of your testimony as a Christian? What kind of witness is it to have people know the price you paid in your health for something as shallow and superficial as breast implants? There is no justification or sense in that.* I gather up all these messages, hold them to my nonexistent bosom, and feel rotten.

Another shame-guilt pattern that sometimes plagues me is what is often called the impostor syndrome. First, the shame voices attack my competence—my skills, ability, intelligence, etc.—by saying, *You know, Marilyn, you don't really know enough about what you're saying to write a book. It's true you have a master's degree in counseling psychology, but that doesn't really qualify you to write about the topics you're tackling here. There are a bazillion books out there covering the same topics you're talking about, and those authors are far more qualified than you. They have Ph.D.'s as well as years of experience in the field.* Then of course the guilt follows. *I'll just quit writing . . . It's true there are many more people more knowledgeable than I . . . Why in the world would I put in all the effort it takes to write this book so the world can find out it's nothing but drivel?*

And that's not all. Shame feeds the impostor voice in yet another realm of my so-called expertise. I have, for the past six years, been one of a six-member speaker team called Women of Faith. We host the largest women's conference in the world; more than one million women have attended our conferences thus far. Along with the other speakers—Patsy Clairmont, Barbara Johnson, Luci Swindoll, Thelma Wells, and Sheila Walsh—I am thrilled to participate in a ministry of such vibrant magnitude. But here's what the shame creep inside says to me: *Marilyn, you're speaking to anywhere from fifteen to twenty-five thousand women every weekend . . . What qualifies you to do that? You're from Amboy, Washington . . . You're no big gun . . . You really ought to go back to the small groups you grew up with . . . The other speakers should be there . . . They have something to say, but not you . . . Next time you open your mouth they're all going to know you don't belong . . . You're a fake. How you ever got here at all is a mystery, but you'd be smart to quit before you're found out.* Now, I'm not incapacitated by these thoughts, but I'd be less than honest if I didn't say they sweep over me from time to time.

There are many more guilt-induced behavior patterns we won't take time to discuss, but let me toss out a few more before we wrap this up. See if you find yourself in one of these:

Guilt carriers are great worriers. Worry comes from fear. Fear comes from not feeling safe. Not feeling safe comes from a shaky love foundation. That lack of foundation produces shame and guilt.

Guilt carriers blame themselves for everything. That's because the guilty person believes there is a fatal flaw deep within herself that effects everyone and everything everywhere. She thinks you'd be smart to get away from her before you get infected.

Guilt carriers continually apologize. They can't bear to inconvenience anyone. Also, since the guilt carrier believes that everyone else thinks she is inefficient and undependable and that whatever she does is not quite right, the least she can do is have the decency to apologize.

Guilt carriers hate for anyone to be mad at them. Nothing is as important as survival to the guilty person, and anger appears to be a direct threat to that survival. To avoid potential anger from other people, the guilt carrier will resort to lying, cheating, or compromising personal standards . . . anything. "Just don't be mad, please!"

Guilt carriers are perfectionists. If her performance can just always be perfect—not just good, but perfect—then the guilty one has so protected her soul that no one will know a stream of shame runs through it.

Hopefully this chapter has made clear that although healthy guilt can be a positive motivator for change, unhealthy guilt, which hooks up with unhealthy shame, can huddle in encampments to the left of the zipper and make us miserable and ineffective. These guilt patterns have the potential to sabotage productivity, stymie development, and silence our authentic voices. When that occurs, we've taken our eyes off of Him who longs to set us free from the bondage of guilt.

Psalm 145:14 states, "The LORD helps the fallen and lifts up those bent beneath their loads" (NLT). Guilt is a heavy load, and the kind of guilt that springs from the toxic shame within us is what the Savior wants to lift from us. As we are willing to look at this guilt, see it for what it is, and participate with God in removing it from our heart's left side, we will have tossed out a toxic tenant that deserves to be forever homeless. Now, that is no tall tale.

Chat Room Possibilities

1. What kinds of experiences make you feel guilty?

2. In these experiences, do you deserve to feel guilty? Is it healthy guilt or unhealthy guilt?

3. Choose a behavior for which you feel shame and determine if it is healthy shame or unhealthy shame. How does knowing the difference help you?

4. How does conscience fit into your ponderings about shame and guilt? How does it help you understand your behavior?

5. What percentage of your waking hours would you guess is spent with feelings of guilt?

Liar, Liar, Pants on Fire!

DETERMINING OUR
PHILOSOPHY OF LYING

Do you have a philosophy of lying? Do you have some yeah buts that would seem to justify occasions when a lie is preferable to the truth?

For example, when you are sure the food at a dinner party must have been catered by Tina's Ptomaine Tavern, the conversation is deadly dull, and you'd prefer to upchuck your meal than listen to one more sentence debating the preferability of Ziploc bags to plastic airtight containers, do you exit the party thanking the hostess for a wonderful evening? Or do you, because of the moral imperatives that guide your life, tell the hostess you are excessively nauseous and will be stopping by the hospital emergency room where in all probability you will die?

When a dear friend who obviously loves her new dress asks if you think it makes her look fat, and the ruffles at the hip line do indeed accentuate a part of the anatomy best left unnoticed, do you say, "No, the dress is flattering," or do you say, "Honey, as quickly as you possibly can you need to return that dress—and stop by Weight Watchers on your way home"?

If your friend bought an outfit, cut off the sales tags, wore the clothes to the event for which it was purchased, and then returned the outfit the next day for a full refund, would you commend her for her practical ingenuity?

On a heavier note, do you deny knowing your friend's husband was seeing another woman because you fear your friend would buckle under the weight of that knowledge?

Do you tell everyone your son is spending the summer with your brother in another state when the truth is he's entering rehab for drug addition?

Consider the woman who tells family and friends that her doctor did not find any problem with the suspicious lump in her breast after all. Why does she withhold the fact that he felt the lump should be biopsied immediately? Is her reasoning that to tell the truth right now would be bad timing in view of "everything else that's going on"?

Were the persons who worked for the underground wrong in lying by protecting Jews during World War II?

What we're pondering here, obviously, is the dilemma of situational ethics. Is lying ever justifiable? There are those who believe that in order to protect human life and dignity, it is at times preferable, even necessary, to lie.

The complex moral issues of lying and truthfulness came to a head for our nation in 1998 as the charges and countercharges surrounding the Clinton administration were televised in graphic detail for all the world to see. When Clinton finally admitted to having "misled" family, colleagues, and the public, great public debate began over the issue of lying being excusable in the context of the humiliating probing of intimate affairs. Many people argued that there is no moral issue at stake when lying to protect personal privacy, especially sexual privacy. Lying under those circumstances is perfectly permissible. Federal Judge Susan Webber Wright helped to bring a measure of closure to these controversies when she found President Clinton in civil contempt of court for having given false and misleading responses designed to obstruct the judicial power.

The Bible, however, does not mince words about lying. It would appear there are no qualifying loopholes that provide the luxury of lying under any circumstance. One of the Ten Commandments is "You shall not bear false witness." Psalm 5:6 states, "Thou dost destroy those who speak falsehood" (NASB). Psalm 58:3 says, "These who speak lies go astray from birth" (NASB). In Colossians 3:9, Paul says, "Do not lie to one another, since you laid aside the old self with its evil practices" (NASB). Jesus said of Satan, "He is a liar, and the father of lies" (John 8:44 NASB).

Saint Augustine maintained that "to use speech for the purpose of deception is a sin. We are not to suppose there is any lie that is not a sin." John Wesley said lies are an abomination to the God of truth. The eighteenth-century philosopher Immanuel Kant maintained that never, ever was it permissible to lie, not even to protect innocent persons from harm.

In contrast, Martin Luther stated in a letter cited by his secretary, "What harm would it do if a man told a good strong lie for the sake of the good and the Christian church . . . a lie out of necessity, a willful lie, a helpful lie, such lies would not be against God; He would accept them." I can't imagine that Luther meant to be taken literally in this statement, but we have no way of knowing if he truly justified such a thing as a "good strong lie." Nevertheless there is great energy surrounding the debate of the "noble" lie. The lies deemed most justifiable are those during situations in which innocent lives are at stake and a lie can deflect the danger.

The "Noble" Lie

My friend Patsy Clairmont told me of an unsettling experience she had a number of years ago at a speaking engagement where a lie saved her from potential danger. She was sharing the platform with Dale Evans, but Dale was not scheduled to speak until sometime after Patsy. As Patsy left the platform and stepped into a darkened hall at the back of the stage, her intent was to make her way back to the auditorium. A man stepped out of the shadows, grabbed her arm, and with great intensity asked, "Where's Dale Evans?" Startled, Patsy pulled her arm back and said, "Dale isn't here yet." He grabbed her arm again and with even greater intensity hissed, "People like you don't understand people like me . . . I never get what I want . . . I have to fight to get what I want, and I want to see Dale Evans."

Patsy was alone in a dark hall backstage with a possibly deranged and increasingly agitated man who began blathering in disconnected phrases about his life of victimization, including being in a hospital for the criminally insane. He had come to see Dale Evans, and he insisted that Patsy had to make that happen.

Terrified but outwardly calm, Patsy assured the man that he would see Dale Evans and just to follow her. As soon as she opened the door into the auditorium lobby, two of the male organizers of the event saw her look of fear and desperation as she was being gripped by a man with dilated pupils and irregular breathing. They immediately came to her aid, stepping between her and the agitated Dale Evans fan. Patsy fled the scene.

The men calmed the man, and he ultimately was seated in the auditorium to see Dale Evans. Patsy, of course, kept an eye on the guy. When he disappeared toward the conclusion of Dale's speech, Patsy alerted the men who had rescued her to check the back door where Dale would exit the stage and where Patsy had been accosted. Sure enough, he was there waiting in the shadows.

Now, here's the question: Was Patsy's lie, that if the man would just follow her he would see Dale Evans, justified? After all, he did get to see Dale Evans as Patsy promised. His assumption, though, was that Patsy was taking him directly to meet Dale Evans personally and not simply to be an anonymous person in the crowd. Some of you reading this might say, "Well, if Patsy had had enough faith she could have trusted God to calm the man down and then presented the plan of salvation to him and he could have prayed to receive Christ right there in the dark hall." Really?

Another type of noble lie is that used by some persons to protect the privacy or confidences of others. For example, a priest is bound by oath to conceal the fact that one of his parishioners is pregnant. He may then feel justified in avoiding questions about her state and of necessity lying to protect her secret. He believes this is his professional obligation. The same sense of professional obligation not to reveal the truth exists with mental health workers, lawyers, and doctors.

Perhaps a more lofty example of the noble lie is smuggling Bibles into countries where the Word of God is not welcome and reading it is, in fact, an illegal act. Or what about those persons who conduct Christian worship services and Bible studies in clandestine settings so as to avoid detection from governments who have outlawed such worship and study? Are they guilty of immorally deceitful practices? Are their good works justifiable in light of God's injunction not to bear false witness?

Let me share with you now, not a noble lie, but a noble disclosure and ask you what would you have done in a similar circumstance. I'm indebted to Dr. Norvel Young's book *Loving Lights Shining Stars* for the story.

Once the father of Immanuel Kant (the philosopher who believed it was never permissible to lie even for noble purposes) was making his way through the heavy woods of Poland to his native country of Silesia. On the road the old man was attacked by a band of thieves who demanded all his valuables. After assuring them he'd given all he had, he was allowed to proceed.

Hurrying away from the scene of this crime, the old man became winded and needed to rest. As he sat down, his hand touched something hard in the hem of his robe. It was gold. He had sewn it there for safety. In his fear and confusion while being robbed he had forgotten about it.

Rushing back to overtake the thieves he breathlessly told them that he had not meant to lie to them when he said they had taken everything he had. He had been too terrified to think at the time, he explained, but once he found the gold in his robe he'd returned so they could take that too if they wished.

The robbers refused his gold. In fact, one of them went to his saddle-bags and retrieved Kant's stolen purse and gave it back to him. Another robber returned Kant's book of prayer, while the last thief led Kant's stolen horse to him and helped him mount it. Then all three robbers asked Kant for his forgiveness and blessing.[1]

Would you have gone back to tell the whole truth and nothing but the truth? If not, why not? If you would have, why? Is this story too far removed from where we live even to have relevance? For whatever it's worth, I'll tell you what I would have done. I'd have hotfooted it through the woods, singing, "Thank You, Jesus, that they didn't find my gold!"—and continued on my way to Silesia dragging my heavy-hemmed robe with me.

Everybody Does It

In Mark Twain's short story "Was It Heaven or Hell?" two tight-lipped, legalistic sisters who saw lying as the worst of all possible sins insist on dragging to the bedside of their exceedingly sick niece her young daughter. The child was forced to confess to her mother that she had committed a horrible sin: She had lied. In sympathy to the child, the doctor in attendance bellowed out: "She told a lie! Did she? God bless my soul! I tell a million a day! And so does every doctor. And so does everybody . . . including you for that matter . . ."

I guess my grandson Alec would agree with the doctor that all people lie. Alec has recently annoyed me to death with his constant singsong

"Liar, liar, pants on fire!" in response to nearly everything he hears. I asked him if he knew what a liar was. He said, "Yeah, it's what Jordan does all day."

"Well, what is that?"

"I don't know, but his pants is on fire!"

For the time being it seemed wise to drop the subject of lying and its consequences for undergarments. I blame all Alec's aberrant behavior on the little pagans he associates with at preschool.

Let's face it: Few of us find ourselves in situations in which we contemplate the need to lie nobly. Most of us don't hide refugees in our tubs and have to choose whether to confess or lie about them to those who pound on the door with the intent of taking them away. Most of us live in the realm of the various "white lies" mentioned at the beginning of this chapter. We assume the lies don't hurt anyone and do occasionally get us off the hook; these are the lies we consider to be well-intentioned. The lies may be told in an effort to flatter, spare another's feelings, cast a cheerful interpretation on depressing circumstances, or show gratitude for unwanted gifts. They may be the lies lovers choose to build each other's egos.

In Shakespeare's sonnet 138, we read about the man and woman who are accepting and pleased with each other's lying—pleased to withhold nothing:

> When my love swears that she is made of truth,
> I do believe her, though I know she lies,
> That she might think me some untutored youth,
> Unlearned in the world's false subtleties.
> Thus vainly thinking that she thinks me young,
> Although she knows my days are past the best,
> Simply I credit her false-speaking tongue;
> On both sides thus is simple truth suppressed.
> But wherefore says she not she is unjust?

And wherefore say not I that I am old?
O, love's best habit is in seeming trust,
And age in love loves not t'have years told.
Therefore I lie with her, and she with me,
And in our faults by lies we flattered be.

White lies are common, and when compared to more threatening lies, it may seem then an overreaction to condemn them. However, Shakespeare's phrase "the world's false subtleties" is mind-arresting because white lies are a part of the world's false face. White lies, though subtle and even seemingly harmless, feed the world's falseness.

The Price of Deceit

Such falseness can start in the home with the white lies we tell our children. For example, how about Santa Claus? Though like the lovers in the sonnet who relished the deceit, what price do we pay when we encourage the deceit of believing in a fat man who delivers presents to every child in the world and, incidentally, whose gifts are based on good performance? (Try teaching Christian grace on the heels of Santa.) When the child grows up enough to realize her parents have been lying, she then loses a sense of trust.

When we adopted our baby, Beth, who was nine days old when she came to our home to "become our daughter," we were told by the Christian adoption agency to tell her the truth about her origins. Their wise counsel was based on the fact that there are too many tragic consequences to adoptees who don't discover they are adopted until late enough in their lives when the news sabotages their security and threatens their identity. In addition, their trust in their adoptive parents is undermined by any well-intentioned deception.

Luci Swindoll has written about her shaken trust when she learned as an adolescent that her adored father had been married before he married Luci's mother. Not only had he been married before, but he also had a son from that first marriage. In Luci's twelve-year-old mind, she had been betrayed—lied to and dishonored. The intent was not to harm Luci by withholding truth from her, but her reaction to this delayed truth was temporarily devastating.

My dear friend Judy Hampton has written movingly in her book *Under the Circumstances* about being seventeen years old, unmarried, and pregnant. She married the baby's father, but of course their baby boy was "born early." In an effort to keep those facts secret, Judy and her husband, Orvie, were not truthful with their son about the year and date of their marriage. When that boy grew to manhood, he discovered the truth and was angry at being lied to as well as deeply troubled at the loss of trust he felt for his parents.

During the latter stages of my husband's pancreatic cancer, Ken asked his doctor if he would live long enough to attend our son, Jeff's, wedding in three weeks. Ken was exceedingly weak and I feared losing him any day, but the doctor answered the question with a cheerful, "Probably." I cornered him in the hall and repeated the question. His truthful answer: "Not a chance." I resented his lie to Ken. It was not a noble lie; it was a weak evasion of the truth, which I found beneath Ken's dignity.

As we drove home from that last doctor's visit, Ken asked me, "I'm not going to make the wedding, am I?"

"No," I said softly. He died a week later.

On a lighter note, what are we communicating to our children when the phone rings and we don't want to talk, so we say, "Answer the phone and tell them I'm not home"? Or how about the note to the teacher saying our child is sick when in reality she's fine but the family wanted to leave a day early for vacation? Is it a problem for Mom to make the elaborate salt map of Siberia for Junior's research project on the life of Alexander Solzhenitsyn? After all, her little fifth grader was "running behind" and couldn't even spell Solzhenitsyn! It may all seem harmless enough on the surface, but when we practice deceit in front of or in conspiracy with our children, we're advocating falsehood and reaping our children's lack of trust in our integrity.

The Fear underneath the Lies

If indeed we assume everyone lies on occasion, the question is why. What motivates a lie? Why is a lie chosen over the truth? I think it all boils down to fear; lies spring from fear. That logic brings Abraham into the picture.

Genesis 12:10–17 recounts how Abraham took his wife and family to live in Egypt in order to avoid the famine engulfing his homeland. Apparently Sarah, his wife, was extraordinarily beautiful. Abraham rightly feared word would reach Pharaoh that a gorgeous woman had come to town but that she was married to a guy named Abraham. Fearing for his life, Abraham instructed Sarah to say she was his sister. Based on that lie Sarah was then taken into the palace of Pharaoh, where she became one of his concubines. Abraham was rewarded with sheep and cattle, male and female donkeys, menservants, maidservants, and camels. When Pharaoh learned Sarah was Abraham's wife, she was released and the couple was told to get out of town!

It was fear that caused Abraham to lie; he feared for his life. It is fear for the lives of others who are threatened that causes us to lie in an effort to defuse the danger. Those kinds of lies we usually consider noble; we say they are well-intentioned.

But fear motivates other lies as well. Most of us fear exposure. Not one of us is proud of all the dimensions of our inner being. We don't want people knowing or seeing our less than honorable ways of being, so we lie for protection. Consider, for example, the doctor who becomes addicted to drugs because of their accessibility and can't risk that exposure, so he uses lies to protect his habit as well as his reputation. The same is true for the person with bulimia. She lies about her binging and purging because exposure might then force her into treatment she doesn't want for a disorder she claims not to have. The pastor who is addicted to pornography cannot risk exposure, so he lies about his behavior and anguishes that he might get caught.

We may also tell lies in an effort to preserve a relationship. For example, prior to marriage, how honest should you be about previous sexual experiences? Should each of you tell all? If knowing that to tell all would be devastating, would it be better to withhold that history? How much of your private history should be allowed to remain private? What about an affair in marriage? Should that be confessed? (See why God spoke out against sexual sin? It makes everything so complicated when we go against the law created for our own good.)

The most gratifying element of an intimate relationship is to be deeply known, fully accepted, and unconditionally loved. To withhold private history because you know your loved one will be deeply hurt and offended creates an air bag between you and your partner. I personally want to be known in intimate relationships with all my secrets, nothing withheld. I can't stand air bags.

However, there is no doubt that we run a risk in that type of transparency. I have seen engaged couples split up over this type of vulnerability as well as marriages put in serious jeopardy when full disclosure was given. In a perfect world where people would love each other as Jesus loves us, we would be safe in telling. Without that best-of-all-worlds environment, however, you may want to weigh the possible consequences before disclosing.

But what about those seemingly harmless "white lies" I mentioned at the beginning of this chapter? Are they too motivated by fear? After all, they're just piddly little falsehoods, right? Let's take a look at them again.

What would motivate us to thank someone for a "wonderful evening" when the Ptomaine Tavern food is threatening to be regurgitated? If we give the impression we've had a great time (which is a lie), how does fear come into the picture? Most of us are highly invested in presenting an image of graciousness. The fear that we will not be viewed as gracious and kind is what motivates the "I-had-a-wonderful-evening" type of lie. That is true in almost all human interaction. We fear the hostess may not like us or respect us unless we flatter her and make her feel good, which of course makes us look good. In this instance, the trick is knowing how to be gracious without lying. It is always honest to thank someone for the time and effort she put into an evening, and it is always honest to thank her for thinking of you.

Let's consider the friend who's crazy about her new dress with hip ruffles. Why would I lie and compliment her on the dress when in reality I'm horrified? Because I fear her displeasure and her disappointment, which I fear may be acted out on me in the form of a pouting morbid silence. My opinion would be rejected and her disappointment would also lead to a rejection of me. That rejection might not last forever, but who wants to ruin a perfectly good lunch while waiting for her to snap out of it? Peace at any price—pass the pizza!

The woman who lies to her family about the suspicious lump the doctor thought should be biopsied fears the responses of her family will be overwhelming. She will have to deal with their emotions as well as her own. That's a double dose of fear she doesn't want to deal with. It feels easier to lie, to put off the disclosure in view of "everything else that's going on."

A Philosophy of Honesty

Let me go back now to the question posed at the beginning of this chapter: Do you have a philosophy of lying? I definitely have a philosophy of lying. With all my heart I believe lying is wrong. However . . . I lie sometimes. Can I justify it? In those cases in which I would lie to protect human life, I am counting on the justification that, as Luther says, it's "a lie out of necessity." However, if and when I lie to protect my image, to cause others to look "less than," or to advance my purposes at the expense of others, I cannot claim the slightest justification and I abhor that behavior.

When I lie, I pay a price. I not only pay the price of a loss of trust from those who know the lie is a lie, but I also lose personal dignity when I lie. There is an inescapable connection between my self-esteem and the degree to which I lie. The deepest problem with lying is that it is in direct opposition to the divine imprint within me. When I don't tell the truth, I lose a measure of personal dignity, which in turn robs me of self-esteem. I lose respect for myself, even if I'm not "caught" in the lie. There is an eroding in my soul that if it had a voice would taunt, "Liar, liar, pants on fire!" The act of lying is in essence a form of treachery against the human spirit.

Do you agree with the doctor in Mark Twain's story that everyone lies? Or do you believe lying is practiced primarily by the pagans surrounding us? Groucho Marx once said there's only one way to find out if a person is honest and does not lie: Ask her. If she says she is honest and never lies, you know immediately you're talking to a liar!

Let me challenge you to reexamine your philosophy of lying. I wonder if we all took greater note of the "innocent" lies we tell, pinpointed the fear behind them, and then addressed that fear, could we not diminish the toxic pileup on the zipper's left side? Not one of us is proud of the lies we tell; that's why we deny them and kick them to the left. Might not becoming more deliberately aware of our deceit and the reasons for it help us kick the habit? I think it's very much worth a try to develop a philosophy—and a practice—of honesty.

Why is that so hard for some of us? In the next chapter we'll explore the subject of fear more deeply and uncover the ways in which fear drives us, not only to lie, but also to present an entirely false identity.

Chat Room Possibilities

1. Do you have a philosophy of lying? Do you find the assumption that everyone lies insulting? Untrue?

2. Do you think lying can become a habit? How have you experienced that habit or seen it in others?

3. This chapter suggests that most lies are motivated by fear. Do you agree? Why or why not?

4. Are you aware of self-esteem loss when you lie?

5. Review Mark 3 and note Jesus' disgust toward legalistic observance of the Law at the expense of human benefit. Does this humanitarian principle apply to the morality of smuggling Bibles?

9

Knock Knock, Who's There?

REMOVING OUR FALSE FRONTS

When my grandson Ian was three years old, he totally discarded his identity and became Peter Pan. He could fly magically about the living room, slicing the air with his sword (Is Peter Pan known to have a sword?), and were I to mistakenly call him Ian, there was a price to pay from the tip of that sword.

Ian, now six years old, has apparently made peace with his identity, and it is currently safe to call him Ian without bodily threat. Last night at dinner, however, four-year-old Alec informed me that he is Batman. I asked him why he is Batman and no longer Alec. His slightly exasperated explanation was that Batman was bad and he wanted to be bad too. This explanation inspired two questions in my mind. Should I explain the duality of little Alec's nature—the side of him that wants to be good and the side that wants to be bad? And do I try to explain that Batman was good, while the Joker was bad? It all seemed far too complex, so I said, "Good night, Batman" as he walked to his mama's car.

We know it is common for children to adopt the identities of those who represent power. Children often feel weak and ineffective. The secretly held power of a Clark Kent who becomes Superman or a Billy who turns into Captain Marvel can provide an escape from feelings of powerlessness.

There are, however, many adults who also suffer from a sense of powerlessness and inadequacy. To compensate, they construct elaborate new identities, which are then presented to the public. The purpose of someone's constructing a new identity is to hide and deny the real one. The real one, which is judged to be weak, flawed, and inadequate, must be kicked to the zipper's left, where hopefully it will remain unnoticed and inactive. The public identity is created out of the need for significance and value.

A blatant example of one who felt it necessary to fabricate a more acceptable, valuable, and significant identity was the southern writer William Faulkner. For most of his youth and early manhood, Faulkner considered himself utterly impotent as a person, and he believed that in order to preserve a sense of self he had to create a new identity.

When the woman he loved jilted him for an officer in the air force, Faulkner determined to become an officer. When he applied for flight training in the United States Air Force, however, he was refused on the grounds that he was undereducated and too short. He applied then to the Canadian Royal Flying Corps. Before filling out the papers, he created an elaborate series of fictions. He claimed that his mother was from Britain; he listed his birthplace as Finchley, Middlesex, and his religion as Church of England.

He never saw active military service but returned to his home in Mississippi with a limp he claimed was a war injury. To his limp Faulkner added the story that he had been wounded in the head. He intimated that with a silver plate in his head, he couldn't be expected to live long. He blamed his heavy drinking on the excessive pain from his war injuries. These fabrications provided for Faulkner a significance missing in his true identity as he viewed it.

One of the greatest terrorists of modern times was Joseph Stalin. The effect of Stalin's neurotic character structure on his career as a revolutionary and on Russian society has been fascinating to scores of biographers. Nikita Khrushchev depicted Stalin as grandiose, insecure, subject to rages, requiring continuous reassurance, arrogant but uncertain, insatiably hungry for glory yet scorning those from whom he received it.

What Stalin did to defend against his deep-seated fear and inadequacy was create a new identity. During the revolution he seized upon a body of materials by which he could shape himself: the writings of Marx and Lenin. Along with the "romance" of revolution, these provided Stalin with purpose and an image of himself as powerful—so powerful, in fact, that he could help overthrow a czar and then replace Lenin, the father of the revolution.

Stalin's real name was Iosif Dzhugashvili. As a child he lived in poverty and was beaten regularly by his drunken father. When Iosif became a man, he found a new name (Stalin means "man of steel"), and he found a new family in communism. He felt he could rescue Russia from victimization by the czar almost as if he imagined the czar to be a drunken father beating his children. But to the left of his new identity festered the old anxiety, self-doubts, anger at authority, and hatred of rivals that fed the young Stalin's anger in the first place.

The Roles We Play

One of the obvious dangers in creating false identities is that we may lose touch with who we really are. An interesting example of this has occurred with the FBI, which increasingly has used undercover agents against drug dealers, terrorist groups, racketeers, and other criminals.

These agents begin by constructing false identities, learning roles, and playacting realities different from their own. There is always danger in undercover work, but an unanticipated danger was showing up with sufficient regularity that FBI officials decided to study the problem: Many agents, once having assumed a false identity, found it difficult to shed the fictions after the undercover assignment was completed. The false role became the true self. The very same elements of personality that make an agent able to play a part are the ones that make it difficult for him or her to shed the role when appropriate.

I have a friend who has difficulty shedding a role. Dixie is hardly an undercover agent, but she presents a false identity in nearly everything she does. For example, she has never especially liked children, including her own. She believes this to be an unacceptable emotion for a mother to feel, so she pretends to love all children. She volunteered as an instructional aide for her son's third-grade classroom, worked in Bible school each summer, and was an aide at her church's primary Sunday-school classes once a month. After all this "practice" at being someone she's really not, even when she's not around children, she gushes and twinkles and exudes childlike enthusiasm. I've told her many times, "Hey, you're with me . . . there's not a child around . . . you can quit simpering." But she can't seem to drop the role.

She is also miserable in her marriage. She basically can't stand her husband, but no one would ever guess it from her behavior. She speaks of him with superlative words and praises. I remember being stunned when she dropped her false role momentarily and confessed her honest desire to bolt out the door and run.

Now, years later, she is simpering over grandchildren who get on her nerves as well as gushing over her husband for whom she still feels little affection. The amazing thing is that her husband has no idea how she feels; I don't know about the grandchildren.

How did Dixie become such a magnificent actress in such a sad and deceitful role? She was raised to believe she had no right to have needs of her own. Her sole role in life was to meet the needs of others. Her mother told her that not only was she to serve others, but she was also to act as if she loved it no matter how she really felt. That's what Dixie's mother did, so that's what Dixie did and still does. Need I tell you Dixie suffers from colitis, lower back pain, and chronic headaches? Dixie has buried her real identity (whatever that might be; she'll probably never know) and assumed the role of one who loves being a wife and mother and has no needs of her own.

Perhaps the most common false identity people construct is what I would call the "whatever-you-want-me-to-be" identity. "Oh, you believe that sugar has a molecular structure that ultimately whittles away the brain's frontal lobe? Well now . . . I guess I'd better cut back on sugar . . . um . . . Does that apply to Almond Joys?" "So, you are picketing in favor of not building this shelter for the homeless because the land is home to the four-clawed, slough-footed lizard? . . . You feel we must make a choice as to who will be homeless? . . . Well yes, you certainly have a point there."

The whatever-you-want-me-to-be identity is motivated by the need to sidestep fear by pleasing others and winning their love and approval. It frequently pops up in a setting of people who don't share our political views or our spiritual convictions. We may justify our silence in such an environment as springing from a desire "not to make waves." Conversely, if we dare to speak up and represent our points of view, we may discover significant pieces of our true identity puzzle.

If Dixie had been present in any of the scenarios just mentioned, she would have remained smilingly silent. She had lived out her fake identity for so long that she wouldn't have a clue what she thought about the four-clawed, slough-footed lizard. In fact, the thought of discontinuing her fiction was downright terrifying to her (much scarier than formulating an authentic lizard philosophy). Pretending had become real to Dixie . . . safe . . . familiar. To do otherwise tapped into a primitive fear that she articulated this way in one of her rare drop-the-facade moments: "If anyone tried to peel back the layers of my behavior in an attempt to reach my core, nothing would be there. There is no 'me,' Marilyn. I have no identity." How very sad . . . and untrue.

One of my favorite fiction writers is Anne Tyler, whose quirky characters consistently make me giggle. They also touch my soul as each tries earnestly and ineffectively to make his or her life work. In Tyler's latest book, *Back When We Were Grownups*, the protagonist, Rebecca, is making breakfast for her husband's ex-wife, Tina, who has flown in from England to attend her daughter's wedding. Rebecca went into a short reverie as she stood motionless over the stove, so Tina impatiently reached over her and grabbed the egg carton to fix her own eggs.

> "It's some kind of cruel joke," Tina said when she had lifted the lid. She was looking down at a double row of eggshells. Rebecca always put the shells back in the carton when she was cooking. In fact, she'd assumed that everyone did. This was what happened when people came to stay: They forced you to view your life from outside, to realize that there was, come to think of it, something faintly mocking about a carton full of empty shells. But two eggs remained intact, and she plucked those out and rapped them against the rim of the skillet.

Many people harbor a secret fear that they are simply empty shells nestled among a carton full of other empty shells. (I guess there's comfort in being surrounded by other empties.) The reality, however, is that not one of us is an empty shell in spite of how we perceive ourselves. Everyone has an identity, even if, like Dixie's, it's been denied and rejected.

Identity Formation

So what is an identity, and how can we be so sure we have one? Our identity is the set of behavioral or personal characteristics by which we are known; it is the distinct personality we all have that sets each of us apart from others. In essence, identity is the stable, consistent, and reliable sense of who one is and what one stands for in the world. It integrates one's meaning to oneself and one's meaning to others.

For example, I do not want a portion of my identity to be that of a silicone-implant survivor. I thank God for His healing interventions in my body, and I attribute my current health and recovery to His graciousness to me. However, I am frequently asked in radio interviews to talk about the effects of silicone and my experience with its toxicity. While I'm willing to respond to the questions up to a point, quite frankly I don't want to be the "poster child" for silicone survivors. Why? I choose to put my energies and focus on issues of emotional and spiritual well-being. I have the option then to shape my public identity to correspond with my personal identity. Identity is fluid, not fixed, and it can be altered according to what inspires us or motivates us.

The process of forming an identity takes place throughout the life cycle, beginning just after birth as we gradually become aware that we have a self. This formation continues to old age when we come to terms with the meaning that self has expressed in terms of spiritual commitments, family interrelatedness, business success and failure, etc. The formation of identity could be envisioned as the assembling of a jigsaw puzzle in which each person has somewhat different pieces to fit together: natural talents, intelligence, social class, physical attractiveness, genetic aspects of temperament, physical limitations, early deprivation or traumatic experiences, as well as positive experiences.

The stage in which identity formation is at its most apparent is adolescence. That's why this stage is so challenging to most parents. Much of adolescence is oriented toward experimentation with possibilities: "Should I drink, chew, or go with girls who do?" "Am I really a conservative like my fuddy-duddy parents, or am I a liberal who should show her true colors by sporting a nose ring and handing out pamphlets that advocate the legalizing of marijuana?" "Do I believe in capital punishment, or should I join the protesters to keep the current death-row inmate alive?" "Do I believe in the biblical account of creation, or did the universe simply happen by chance?" The list of possibilities is endless. So too is the pressure on the adolescent to come to terms with her warring complexities in an effort to form an identity that "fits."

The sobering thing for parents gripping the corners of their chairs as this whole drama unfolds is that choices that produce traumatic consequences become a part of our identity. Various traumas and poor choices can never be undone. Our poor choices can certainly be forgiven, but they do leave a permanent imprint.

What is encouraging about the formation of identity is that the self can always be modified. We are capable of insight that can lead to healthier choices than we may have originally made. Stalin, for example, though the object of his father's drunken rages, had a choice in how to develop his identity. So too did Faulkner. But each saw the construction of a false identity as the solution to his powerlessness. Dixie also had choices. She did not have to live out her mother's identity; she was born with a uniqueness that did not program her into a preset code of behavior. But it seemed easier to her to live a life of flat and uninspired conformity.

When we realize that we do not have to continue to be as we have been, that we can consider revisions and try out new possibilities, we are encouraged to discontinue presenting the false identity. There are *real* options available to us. We can reclaim our birthright.

Reclaiming Our True Self

A child in Harriet Beecher Stowe's *Uncle Tom's Cabin* was asked, "Do you know who made you?" She speculated, "Nobody, as I knows on," said the child with a short laugh . . . "I 'spect I jist grow'd."

But the Bible says something very different. One of my favorite verses in Scripture is Jeremiah 1:5: "Before I formed you in the womb I knew you." That is a mind-boggling thought. Before I was ever in the womb of my mother, I was in the mind of my sovereign Creator. What does that mean? God apparently mused, pondered, and thought about my essence and my identity before He called me into being. I am not a composite of haphazardly thrown-together molecules, traits, and characteristics.

God deliberated in the same way, painstakingly and lovingly, over the formation of each of us. We are persons of great complexity and enormous potential, thoughtfully and deliberately formed by the Almighty. We are not creations who "jist grow'd."

The recognition of our God-given potential to formulate and reformulate our identity is of enormous importance as we consider whether we have a discarded self whom we perceive to be weak, powerless, and inadequate. If indeed we are divine creations who are given freedom to modify our identity, then we don't need to have that secret self giving off fumes to the left of the zipper. When we call it out of hiding and then examine why it feels inadequate, weak, and powerless, we've begun the process of healing. Our true self was not created to live with a sense of inferiority. That self was not created to compensate for powerlessness by becoming angry, cruel, and controlling. Rather, that self was created for the inhabitation of the God of the universe, who says, "Behold, I make all things new" (Rev. 21:5). We can change; we can become new creatures! It is the plan of God that we live out of the true self that is able to be restored and made whole in the image of our Creator.

God also assures our anxious hearts through his prophet Jeremiah in 29:11–12, "'For I know the plans that I have for you,' declares the LORD, 'plans for welfare and not for calamity to give you a future and a hope. Then you will call upon Me and come and pray to Me, and I will listen to you'" (NASB). God's promise is to listen as we pour out the pain that called our false selves into being in the first place. He promises that His plan for us is a life of hope, not despair. If we take Him at His word, our future looks bright as the false self yields to the formation of our identity based on God's love for us as well as His divine plan for us.

God walks freely throughout our whole self. He does not see us as "zippered" or inadequate or unlovable. He does not reject our true self in favor of whatever facade we've been hiding behind. What a comfort to know that we do not need to be afraid to be who we really are.

Chat Room Possibilities

1. What words would you use to describe your identity?

2. What childhood experiences do you think shaped your identity?

3. What part of your identity has changed in the last five years?

4. Are there facets of your current identity you would like to change? How will you do that?

5. What environment tempts you to present a false self?

10

You're Really Tickin' Me Off

DEVELOPING A HEALTHY
SENSE OF ANGER

There is an unusual lizard (that looks very much like an iguana) that has a decidedly off-putting way of communicating the "you're-really-tickin'-me-off" message. Whenever this reptile is either frightened or angry, it constricts a muscle in its neck, closing off its jugular vein. As a result of that constriction, the lizard's blood is prevented from returning to its heart. Instead, it wells up in the reptile's head, causing it to swell. Its eyes bulge as if they are about to pop out, and finally the pressure becomes so intense that a very fine stream of blood is discharged from an agglomeration of blood vessels at the corner of each eye. The squirting range is about six feet. Mixed with the blood is an irritant that causes all within range to deeply regret having ticked off the lizard.

I had a science teacher in junior high school who seemed to have a similar capability of communicating, "You're really tickin' me off." He didn't squirt blood mixed with a noxious irritant, but his eyes bulged, his face turned red, and I'm sure his head doubled in size. Not one of us wanted to be in range when he grew into his "condition." What usually set him off was any challenge to his authority. He was also the boys' basketball coach, and "stupid mistakes" incited the lizard syndrome on the court.

Why do people and events tick us off? Why do we get so mad sometimes? Let's swing to the first woman puttering about in the Garden of Eden. As we know, all of Eve's needs were met. She had security, limitless food, leisure, environmental beauty, love, and perfection! However, God had placed one simple restriction on her behavior: She could have nothing to do with the tree of the knowledge of good and evil. Scripture does not tell us she chafed under that directive, but she was certainly receptive to the evil one's suggestion to flex against that divine no-no. The reality is, human beings don't like someone to tell us we can't do something. It makes us rebellious . . . It can really tick us off!

Yesterday, Beth and the children and I were on a little outing. Alec, who just turned four last week and is immensely proud of the fact, told his mom, "Don't say no to me." A few minutes later he said, "You're not the boss of me." Developmentally we know that four-year-olds can be maddeningly determined to test boundaries and assume control of their own lives. It ticks them off when they can't. But interestingly enough, most of us remain at that stage of "Don't say no to me" and "You're not the boss of me" no matter how old we are.

The Power Struggle

One of the origins for feeling ticked off is a desire for control. Losing control over a life circumstance or losing control over a person becomes a power issue. This principle is true even of the lizard. He becomes angry because of a threat to his well-being. The threat is lack of control in providing for his own safety, loss of necessary power for his survival. This primitive need for power and control exists in all God's creatures.

Why does a child have a tantrum? Because she is not getting what she wants when she wants it. She has no control, she has no power, but she does have lungs so she uses what is available to her. Her goal? To get the adult power-holder to surrender. If and when there is a surrender, the child has gained control and the tantrum is over . . . until the next power struggle ensues.

The quest for power and control exists in the sandbox too. Dexter has more Tonka trucks that Vladimir, who is ticked off about that. Vlad takes three of Dexter's trucks and lines them up behind his own. Dexter's temperament, the modeling he's observed in anger management at home, and the degree to which the loss of three trucks motivate him to declare war will determine who maintains control in the sandbox. Sandbox mentality prevails in world affairs. "You took my country and I won't stand for it. I'll fight you, even kill you, to get it back."

When our teenager leaves the house with purple perpendicular hair and a nose ring, in all probability a power struggle occurred before the front door was opened. Guess who surrendered?

When couples come for therapy claiming "irreconcilable differences," those issues are frequently power and control issues. It can start with benign arguments about his relentless switching of TV channels each night or her hours spent on the phone instead of sitting with him enjoying the flashing, jerking TV images made possible by the infamous clicker. How to raise the children, how to manage the money, where to go on vacation, how long the mother-in-law can stay in the guest room, whether to buy a new car, why sports are so important . . . all are issues of control. When she believes it should be done her way and he believes it should be done his way, they are in a power struggle. The one who does not get his or her way is the one who gets angry.

Being ticked off doesn't always escalate to the lizard syndrome. But when it does, anger can be frighteningly forceful in its destructiveness.

Yesterday I read in the paper about a man who in a rage killed his two children, his wife, and then himself. He left a note of explanation stating that life was unfair and the world too hard a place in which to live. A background check revealed he had lost his job a month prior to the murders and his wife had filed for divorce. Slaughtering everyone gave him a sense of regaining control of his life—getting his power back—even though it cost him his life!

Park Dietz, a forensic psychiatrist who has interviewed numerous school shooters, has been quoted in *Time* magazine as saying the shooters have a number of characteristics in common: depression, anger, access to weapons, and a violent role model. The article goes on to state that almost all the shooters were expressing rage, either against a particular person for a particular affront or, more often, against a whole bunch of bullying classmates. The bullying robbed the shooters of their sense of power and control. Killing, to their way of thinking, restored the balance of power.

After Jacob Davis used a magnum bolt-action rifle to mow down his girlfriend's ex-lover at his Tennessee high school in 1998, he dropped down beside the bleeding body. A friend came over and said to Davis, "Man, you just flushed your life down the toilet." Davis replied, "Yeah, but it's been fun." He too thought his revenge restored the balance of power. He is now serving a fifty-two-year term at a medium-security correctional facility. Before the shooting, he had received an academic scholarship to study computer science at Mississippi State University. Contrary to his intent, when he lost control of his behavior, he lost all control of the events of his life.[1]

Healthy Hissing

We can recognize that anger is used to restore power and regain control, but just what is anger? Most of us have an understandable fear of unleashed anger because we see its destructiveness among nations, between family members, and within ourselves. Our contemporary ideas about anger are based on the belief that inside every tranquil soul is a furious one screaming to get out. When it gets out, we often read about it in the papers.

Are we really all housing a monstrous lizard within us that is capable of destroying the universe? I say no, we are not. As Neil Clark Warren points out in his book *Make Anger Your Ally,* anger is simply a physical state of readiness. When we get angry, more adrenaline is secreted in our body, more sugar is released, our heart beats faster, our blood pressure rises, and the pupils of our eyes dilate. We are on the alert and, as a result, all the power of our person is available to us. The purpose of this biological mechanism is to come to our aid when our survival is threatened. If we had no capacity for anger, then we would be incapable of protecting ourselves and asserting ourselves in the world. We would be virtually helpless in the face of difficulty requiring strength. When such power is used positively, it can preserve life and secure the environment.

There is a winsome old fable the intent of which is to teach us the need for self-preservation. It goes something like this:

Once upon a time on a path that went by a village in Bengal there lived a cobra whose habit it was to slither out of hiding and bite the people on their way to worship. After a short period of time the people stopped going to the temple because they feared being bitten on the way.

The priest of the temple became aware of the problem and sought out the cobra for a chat about its behavior. The priest pointed out that it was wrong to bite the people who walked along the path to worship and convinced the cobra never to engage in that behavior again.

As time passed the people realized the cobra had stopped its biting so they lost their fear and resumed their walk on the path. Soon it became known that the snake had not only stopped biting but was passive as well. The village boys began dragging the snake about, bashing it against rocks, and basically taunting it mercilessly.

The temple priest passed along the path one day and called out to the snake to see if it had kept its promise. The battered and bruised snake came out of hiding and laboriously made its way to the priest. When the priest saw the condition of the snake, he asked what had happened. In tears the cobra said he had been abused ever since he made his promise to bite no more. The priest's response was, "I told you not to bite, but I did not tell you not to hiss."

A number of years ago our good friend Randy was shopping in a grocery store with his daughter. When he realized that his three-year-old was no longer by his side, he tore around the aisles calling her name. Others in the store joined him in his frantic search. Thinking she might have wandered outside, he dashed to the front door and saw a man shoving his little girl into the backseat of a green Buick. Yelling, Randy ran to the car and literally pulled the door off the hinges as the driver attempted to speed away. Randy grabbed the driver, threw him to the ground, and then pulled his daughter out of the car and into his arms. Three men (other shoppers) surrounded the kidnapper and kept him on the ground while a woman called the police on her cell phone. There was a lot of good, healthy hissing going on in that scene. That state of biological readiness probably saved the life of Randy's child.

I read a newspaper account of biological readiness that went at least one step beyond hissing. Please forgive the indelicate subject, but it's too pertinent not to share it with you. The newspaper account stated that a man has been charged with trying to rape a woman who castrated him during an alleged attack. A twenty-one-year-old man tried to force a forty-two-year-old woman to perform a sex act on him. While the two struggled, the woman bit off his testicles. The woman went to police headquarters and turned the testicles over to officers. The police said the rapist later arrived at a local hospital with injuries matching the woman's description. Doctors were unable to reattach his testicles. The rapist remained in the hospital in police custody and was listed in stable condition.

I guess there are times when hissing must be followed by a well-placed bite!

Responding Responsibly

Clearly, anger itself is not a bad thing. It is, in fact, a part of the equipping God gave to us to aid in coping with hurtful, frustrating, and fearful experiences. Learning to manage this God-given capability will help us in dealing with the pain in our lives and even some of the injustices of the world in which we live. For example, we first feel anger when we hear and read about child victimization, world hunger, ethnic cleansing, abortion, prejudice . . . the list goes on. Our indignation spurs us in the direction of participating in the solving of these social ills. The challenge, of course, is learning positive ways to harness that energy from anger, to redirect it in ways that are not detrimental to ourselves and society.

With that goal in mind, let's add more insight about anger to our storehouse of knowledge. I don't agree with Sigmund Freud, who shaped our view of anger as being a monstrous instinct that lives within each of us. Our responses to anger can reflect the depravity of the human soul, and to the degree we yield to that depravity by responding to circumstances with mean and hurtful angry reactions, we are living out of that depravity. That can look monstrous. However, we have a choice in how to respond to what threatens to set off the lizard syndrome. We need not be helpless victims. That's good news!

There are ways to relearn and rethink angry responses. That relearning and rethinking can save marriages and improve parent-child relationships as well as every other interaction we experience in a world inhabited by people who have the potential to tick us off. When we understand what has caused us to become angry, we can formulate a strategy for dealing with our anger before it becomes an aggressive behavior . . . before we start spurting blood and poison.

Your response may be, "Well, I can tell you exactly what makes me angry. It's my husband . . . the kids . . . the boss . . . slow drivers . . . that insipid blonde bank teller who makes accounting errors and wanly blames me . . . the crabby way my neighbor looks at me. . . the woman at the cleaners who chastises me for bringing in clothes with stains of unknown origins . . . waiting in line . . . the people who tell me to calm down when they're the ones who got me mad in the first place!"

Most of us assume that we would be loving, pleasant citizens if it were not for all those people and events that destroy our tranquillity and cause our heads to begin swelling. We think, *If it weren't for . . . I'd be . . .*" But deep down we know that blaming others for how we feel or act is a cowardly bit of scapegoating that solves nothing. It just perpetuates the problem of being continually ticked off. So what's the answer?

To begin with, we have to take responsibility for our behavior and not blame others. That means that even though the insipid blonde bank teller is wildly annoying, our responses are under our control. We have a choice. We can offer the person arsenic tea . . . or a courteous word and a smile. Now admittedly this thinking has as much appeal as spending a morning with Martha Stewart making bird feeders out of pine cones. We want to react, pay back, punish behavior that hurts us. (So did the school shooters.) But that formula does not work, and it is not God's plan. So our task is to formulate a strategy for dealing with our anger that is built upon the foundation of knowing we have a choice in how we behave. We don't have to let our anger escalate into the lizard syndrome.

Myths about Anger

In formulating a strategy for dealing with anger constructively, let's first get rid of a few myths about anger. In so doing, we won't be tempted to include the myths in our strategy.

To begin with, people often assume aggression and anger are the same, but they are not. Anger is a neutral state of preparedness; aggression is a behavior. The intent of aggression is to assault or attack. Whether the aggression is verbal or physical, it is always designed to punish or do harm. The school shooters have all been described as angry. A more accurate description would be that they were angry and chose to express that anger in aggressive ways (violence and murder). Anger was their neutral state, but aggression was their destructive behavior. This is an important distinction because when we understand what has put us into the anger state, we can formulate a strategy for dealing with it before it becomes an aggressive behavior.

Another helpful distinction to make has to do with being assertive. Assertion is not aggression. When we are assertive, we express our feelings, needs, or opinions in a forthright manner but without the goal of hurting. Assertion is merely communicating the truth as we see it without diminishing, criticizing, or insulting the hearer by our words. Assertion leaves room for differences of opinion that are fairly expressed. Though assertion may have its root in anger, it is a positive way of expressing anger.

A negative way of expressing anger is through hateful hostility. How many times have you heard your child or someone else's child scream, "I hate you!"? Worse yet, how many times have you heard your spouse say that or a friend or a relative? To scream, "I hate you" requires that we know what hate is. To understand hate, we must understand hostility.

Hostility is an attitude. Generally a hostile person has a negative attitude that reflects an embittered soul full of animosity toward life and others. The hostile person has not learned to use anger effectively and feels pessimistic about his or her ability to change his life circumstances. Hate is hardened hostility. Like hostility, hate becomes progressively more negative in relation to another person or group of persons. The school shooters were hostile and consumed with hatred.

Neil Clark Warren breaks down these distinctions and charts their development in the following helpful list:

1. First, we feel hurt, frustration, or fear (and, I would add, loss of control).

2. As a reaction to these, we become physiologically aroused in order to deal with whatever has hurt, frustrated, or threatened us. This is anger.

3. If our expression of anger over time fails to be effective, we are left with a residue of resentment. A collection of resentment leads to a generally negative attitude about life. This attitude of negativity and pessimism is hostility.

4. As hostility hardens, it becomes hate. Hate is usually felt toward that person whom we perceive to be the cause of our own hurt, frustration, or threat but with whom our anger has been ineffective in producing any change. If we now hate that person, we probably have lost hope of any resolution.[2]

This is a sobering progression of emotion, but the God-given survival instinct of anger need not become an enemy if we understand it and learn how to refocus and rechannel it in ways that are not destructive.

Another widespread myth about anger is that if a person is allowed or helped to express it, he will in some way benefit from it. This belief occupies a position of central importance in almost all psychotherapies. We are encouraged to "get it off our chests," "blow off steam," or "let it all hang out." Sports or strenuous physical activities are praised as a means of "working off" feelings, especially hostility, and it is generally accepted that there is some value in hitting, throwing, or breaking something when frustrated.

Early on in my work as a counselor I was dealing with a woman who appeared to be a literal walking Vesuvius of anger. She was sixty-five years old, had been married to two exceedingly abusive men (both of whom died), and had been raised by parents who were cruel, insensitive, and volatile. My client, whom I'll call Ginger, had never had therapy before. I had been trained to believe that our first task was to "siphon off" her anger level. I suggested she go to a local thrift store and buy some dishes, fling them one at a time at the concrete brick wall in the backyard, and yell out anything that came to mind as she did so.

This activity proved so satisfying to Ginger that she ultimately bought out the china supply of every thrift store in her area. However, her wild flinging and yelling brought complaints from her neighbors. Their complaints made her furious. Oddly enough, her venting only fed the need for more venting. I finally suggested we take a different approach to her anger. I feared she might kill a neighbor or they her.

In my training I accepted the commonly held Freudian view that aggression is an inherited destructive drive that is literally built into the very nature of a person. I have only recently realized how unfair it is to each of us to assume we are programmed for beastly violence and that to counteract that drive we must find some physical catharsis to put us in a less volatile state. More and more studies are revealing that raging, violent responses are learned behaviors, not inherent determinants.

Other studies show that venting anger is not only ineffective, but it actually feeds aggression. This includes fantasized aggression. Ginger became increasingly volatile the more dishes she flung. Had we not switched strategies, the entire neighborhood might have been reduced to a raging community of dish slingers. Letting off steam is great if you're a teapot, but for a person it merely produces more steam. This has sobering implications for our children because the more aggression they watch on television or see in their home, the more aggression they are inclined to express.

One of the first studies to take issue with the get-it-off-your-chest tactic was conducted by Seymour Feshbach in 1956. He put together a group of boys who were not aggressive or destructive and encouraged them to play with violent toys, kick the furniture, and do whatever wild things they could think of during a series of free-play hours. This freedom to act out destructively did not "drain" any of the boys' aggression or pent-up anger. What the study revealed is that the boys developed a greater inclination toward angry behavior.

In another study in which third-grade children were frustrated and irritated by another child, the children were given one of three ways of "handling" their anger: Some were permitted to talk it out with the adult experimenter, some were allowed to play with guns for "cathartic release" or to "get even" with the frustrating child, and some were given a reasonable explanation from the adults for the child's annoying behavior. Which "remedy" was most effective in dispelling their anger? Not talking it out or playing with guns (the latter, in fact, made them more aggressive), but understanding why their classmate had behaved as she did (she was sleepy, upset, sick).

These same principles of anger and aggression apply to adults. Couples who yell at each other do not feel less angry, but more angry. Verbal aggression and physical aggression are only one short step from each other.

A Strategy for Handling Anger Effectively

So what's the best strategy for dealing with anger? First, we remember we are not victims inherently programmed for aggression. Venting, spewing, hitting, and raging do not get rid of aggression, but escalate it. In our state of physical readiness, we have a choice in how we respond to the various anger triggers that set us off.

With this in mind, the first step I would suggest is that we know what sets us off. What consistently seems to raise our blood pressure and threaten to send our eyes into a state of pop? The value of knowing is that we can stop the emotion before it affects the jugular.

For example, perhaps you're extremely sensitive to criticism (no one likes criticism, but some people find it a seemingly uncontrollable anger trigger), and during lunch your friend Sue starts in on you about your behavior at the neighborhood barbecue. Because you have started a diary chronicling what ticks you off, you're aware of how easily, quickly, and frequently criticism sets you up for an angry response. Now hearing your friend's criticism, you realize what your usual response would be (shove your Chinese chicken salad in her face with the hope that a few mandarin oranges might be ingested, thus blocking her air passages). So you know in advance to monitor your reaction. (More on monitoring shortly.)

As you keep your anger record, I suggest noting these facts: What was the intensity of the anger? How long was I ticked off (five minutes, two hours, four months)? How did I respond? What did I do? The benefit of keeping a record is that we begin to see a pattern to our anger. Perhaps it occurs in specific situations, with specific people, or under specific circumstances. We can see then that the anger is not entirely in the "self," but in the situation. As a result, the solution becomes clearer. For example, if your diary indicates that certain people are consistently toxic to you, you may need to see them less frequently. If they are always critical, demeaning, negative, and hurtful, you may need to stop seeing them altogether. The diary will hopefully help you know what you are angry about.

The next step is to ask yourself the crucial question, "What do I want when I get mad?" There's always "a want" in our anger, and we need to know what it is. For example, on a negative note, what we want from our anger may be to hurt the person who has hurt us. Or perhaps we want that person to feel guilty. Perhaps in our revenge state we want to humiliate the person and in so doing communicate what a jerk he or she is. We want our power back.

Let's swing back and consider my plate-slinging client, Ginger. What purpose did her anger serve? She came to realize that what she wanted was to be loved, esteemed, and valued—responses she had never received. She was angry because she had been cheated out of those reasonable love experiences. However, her anger didn't gain for her what she wanted. Her anger kept her churning on a treadmill of resentment and often hostility. (She moved to a different neighborhood only to find that environment no more loving than the one she left . . . even though she no longer threw plates.)

Basically, we all want what Ginger wanted. We want to be valued, loved, and made to feel uniquely special. We want to be heard, understood, and treated as one worthy of negotiating with when differences occur. We don't want differences to divide and alienate us from each other. We want to live in harmony and peace where the atmosphere is one of mutual respect. What happens when we don't experience that? It ticks us off!

After you've kept a record of your anger responses, the next step is to be on the alert for the trigger that sends that feeling of anger charging down your nerve pathways. When you feel it coming, shout, "Stop!" to yourself. Do not under any circumstances respond! Delay . . . buy time . . . wait. Your intent now is to break the habit of your anger response. Tell yourself you are in control and you need a minute or two to figure out how you're going to handle the situation. Thomas Jefferson suggested counting to one hundred as a delay tactic; Mark Twain said count to ten . . . and if that doesn't work, swear. (No, no.)

The second step is to reinterpret the trigger event. For example, the insipid blonde bank teller who drives us crazy may be suffering from a rare form of leukemia and she's on her third medication. The side effect of that medication is insipidness! If while we buy time we think out any number of possible reasons for her behavior, all of which cause us to feel bad for her, we've reinterpreted her behavior, which causes our anger to diminish and our empathy to elevate.

Here's another example of how empathy changes what we think and then feel. Let's assume I'm in an extremely crowded elevator—

people-packed to the point of immobility. As we're crawling to my destination on the twentieth floor, I am being poked and prodded by someone behind me. I am infuriated by the inappropriate poking but remain helplessly rooted to my tiny elevator space because I can't move. But the minute I reach the twentieth floor, I leap out and wheel around with the intention of delivering an angry, scathing address to the "poker" who took advantage of me in cramped quarters. However, now that I'm looking at him, I realize he is blind. He's leaning on his stick, moving it around slightly in an effort to maintain his balance.

The elevator doors close and it continues its slow climb to who knows where. I begin my slow descent from boiling mad. What happened to my anger? It was reinterpreted. What I think dictates what I feel. There was no way I could be angry at the blind man. I interpreted him differently once I realized he was trying to maintain his balance on the elevator and not poke me inappropriately. The mind is a powerful ally in helping us control anger. Feelings have no brains. They simply communicate our interior states of being; they don't include logic and reason or suggestions for how to manage those states of being.

This reappraisal method is being used with people who are exposed to constant provocations as part of their jobs. For example, New York City has a program that teaches city bus drivers that passengers who have irritating mannerisms may actually have hidden handicaps. The elderly man who repeatedly asks if they've come to Eighty-third Street yet may have Alzheimer's; the seemingly drunk woman in seat seven may be exhibiting symptoms of cerebral palsy; petit mal epileptic seizures can make a passenger seem to be deliberately ignoring a driver's orders. The bus drivers say these new insights reduce the arousal of their anger; they no longer assume they are under attack once they reinterpret the motives of their passengers.

The next step after cooling off and reinterpreting is communicating.

Unfortunately, most people don't know how to express anger without attacking or belittling. There's the verbal aggression style ("You jerk, how could you do that to me?") contrasted with the reporting style ("I was really mad when you just left me at the party to talk to a bunch of people I don't know . . . I felt insecure and nervous.") Verbal aggression usually fails because it riles up the other person and causes him or her to be inclined to strike back. The reporting style gives a description of your state of mind that constitutes less of an attack. Thomas Gordon, the originator of Parent Effectiveness Training, calls this the difference between I-messages and you-messages.

The most effective communication uses I-messages ("I feel . . ."; "It appears to me that . . ."; "It hurts me when . . .") in a gentle voice. Raising your voice is counterproductive. Remember, yelling feeds aggression. The careful preservation of each person's dignity is also imperative. Assume the person you're talking with has a worthy side; listen without interrupting, sighing, rolling your eyes, or making mouth noises. (Mouth noises drive me crazy.) Then let the other person state his or her position with the same civility. Be sure you've each heard the other's viewpoint and understood what that viewpoint is.

The final step in successfully handling anger is to solve the problem! Our anger has put us in a state of readiness to make a grievance known. Dissenting views have had the opportunity to be communicated without aggression. So far, so good.

So let's pick up on lunch between you and Sue. You're munching on your respective Chinese chicken salads. Sue has finished criticizing you. The burden of communicating hurt feelings (or intense anger if we want to be accurate) rests upon you. You know you're angry and you know why. What you want is for Sue to say that contrary to what she had first said, you were really a doll at the barbecue and there was no reason for her to have criticized you. Not an option; Sue doesn't offer. Based on everything you've just read, how should you proceed? What should you say and how should you say it? Could you opt to say nothing at all? If yes, why? If no, why? What do you want from Sue (besides her picking up the lunch tab)?

The Source of Real Power

Now let's talk about my golf game. (How's that for giving you whiplash?) My son-in-law, Steve, is a golf pro. His greatest strength is as a teaching pro; he has helped hundreds of people improve their games and lower their scores. When Beth and Steve were first married, I took advantage of having a golf pro in the family and asked him if he'd help me eliminate the hook and slice in my drive. (I can do both in an easy succession of moves.) He patiently showed me what was wrong with my grip and reminded me of the need to reposition my feet and shoulders and to keep my head down until the shot was completed. With the new grip and body positioning in mind, he told me I would need to practice the shot thirty times in succession in order to put my new positioning in muscle memory. Guess what? I still have an erratic hook and slice. Is that because Steve gave me poor advice? No, it's because I didn't practice. I meant to . . . it just seemed like too much work . . . too much time. *So what's wrong with a hook or slice?* I asked myself. *No big deal.* (Yes, I still have a bad drive.)

I've heard people say, "Yeah, I went to therapy for a while. It didn't do me any good . . . Nothing's changed . . . It's a waste of time and money if you ask me!" Whether it's golf, therapy, or learning to ski, we must be willing to learn and then practice the skills. The same is true with anger management. Deeply entrenched habits take work to change, but it is possible as well as rewarding.

However, as much as I believe in the value of our efforts to relearn patterns that produce bad habits and as much as I believe in the tools for change made possible through psychology, there is an unmistakably powerful component for change that only God provides. Let me tell you Stanley's dramatic story.

Stanley was a highly respected community leader and church partici-
pant. His astute business mind had produced several multimillion-
dollar companies. He gave generously of his time and money. One
summer he spent a month in Guatemala rebuilding homes in an area dev-
astated by an earthquake. He appeared to have a heart for human need.

It didn't fit the picture then when his wife and two teenage daughters
literally fled from home one night and flew to the wife's parents' house
several states away. Stanley was immediately surrounded with loyal
supporters who sympathized with him over his loss. When he told the
church board of his wife's mental instability, everything seemed to fall
into place. Stanley's base of support grew.

What the people didn't know was that Stanley was prone to uncontrollable rages. He would beat his daughters with a belt and his
wife with his fists. They lived in terror of setting him off. For years the
wife's parents had begged her to leave. She hesitated because she had
no "biblical grounds" for leaving. Finally, however, in desperation she
and the girls fled.

Three months later, Stanley was rocked to the core of his being. He
was sitting in his customary pew one Sunday morning when the pastor
was preaching about the meaning of Jesus' statement, "You will know
them by their fruits." Stanley had prided himself on his "fruit": support
to the community, his church, and even the world. He gave generously
of himself and his money; he was pleased with himself. But God was not.

Suddenly, without warning, Stanley saw himself as God saw him: a
secretly violent, hateful man. The fruit of the Spirit is love. Stanley was
not filled with love; he was filled with inexplicable rage and hostility.

The pastor suggested that many people believe their good deeds
will get them into heaven, but the only entrance to heaven comes
from a confession of personal sin and then receiving Christ as Savior.
Fruit then is produced as a result of that salvation experience; love is
one of those fruits. Stanley had grown up in the church; what he
heard that Sunday morning was not new to him. But God did a

"Damascus Road" number on Stanley. Stanley realized for the first time that he was not a Christian. He was trying to look like one, but in his heart he saw himself as God saw him: aggressive, hateful, violent, and totally without love for anyone.

The conviction of the Holy Spirit was so powerful to Stanley that he met with the pastor for three hours after the service. Sobbing, he confessed his need of a Savior, his violent behavior toward his wife and daughters, and his complacency and pride about his many "good works." He confessed his stubborn refusal to yield to any power greater than his own. He admitted that he compensated for his bad behavior by doing good things, but that those things were always his choice and under his control. He lived for control. However, on that Sunday morning he yielded control to the God he'd heard about all his life but never known personally.

Stanley's life began to show fruit—real fruit. He begged his wife's forgiveness on the phone and told her he had started therapy as well as a weekly meeting with his pastor. He confessed to his daughters and asked for their forgiveness.

After so many years of abuse, it took time for sufficient trust to be built so the wife and daughters felt safe in returning. But six months later, the family reunited. Stanley was a different man. Why? He did conscientious work with his therapist on anger management and remained humbly accountable to his pastor. But his ultimate healer was God. God did a bright-light number on Stanley; he became a new creature.

I worked with Stanley's wife and two daughters shortly after their return. The years of abuse left deep scars. Both girls continue to have trust issues with men as well as problems with self-esteem. Stanley's wife has struggled for years with a low-grade depression; we had to attend to that as well as her lack of self-confidence. Through it all, however, God is proving to be present to each member of this family. For years, the girls felt God had turned His back. Now they're slowly beginning to see His face.

I've included this chapter on anger in the left-hearted lodgers section because unmonitored anger responses are becoming an increasingly serious problem for our society. We don't want it known that we have an aggression problem, so once again we deny the behavior and kick it to the zipper's left. Sadly, there are many Stanleys out there who refuse to face up to the sin of their aggressive behavior. As a result, marriages are breaking apart, children are fearful and insecure, and many in American society are engulfed in rage.

God desires a spirit surrendered to His will. His will is that we experience wholeness—no longer split in two by the zipper that causes us to lead a double life, but deeply healed by His power. What a comfort it is to know that God is not passively leaving us to our duplicity, but He continues to do a Damascus Road number on people on a regular basis. As far as I can see, the only lasting solution for our society is many more bright-light knockdowns.

Chat Room Possibilities

1. What is the value of anger? Of what benefit can anger be to you?

2. Was Jesus' anger at the moneychangers in the temple an example of anger, aggression, or assertion? Was it none of those three emotions?

3. Have you ever come close to experiencing the lizard syndrome? What set you off?

4. Is anger a sin?

5. Are you aware of what ticks you off? Is there a pattern? Are you more angry with others or more angry with yourself?

I Just Can't Seem
to Stop Myself

OVERCOMING ADDICTIONS

I have recently learned that prostitution runs rampant in Antarctica. One might assume that because there are no McDonald's, movie theaters, or Dunkin' Donuts, perhaps entertainment potential is at a minimum, thus giving rise to an activity that might offer circulatory warmth as well as monetary reward. But this prostitution is not among human beings. It is instead occurring among the Adélie penguins on Ross Island, 650 miles from the South Pole.

Now, I don't know why this knowledge gives me a giggle except for the fact that penguins always inspire giggles in me. But beyond that response I find the following facts fascinating.

What these enterprising little feathered floozies do is have close fellowship with males other than their spouses in exchange for stones.

Once the favor has been bestowed, the female is given a stone; she puts it in her beak and then waddles home to her unsuspecting spouse. What is practical about this is that hundreds of stones are needed to build the average nest. Mama's lack of moral fidelity might be rationalized away by pointing out that were it not for her moonlighting, there would be foundational instability in her home.

The winsomeness of penguins and the study of their sexual patterns does not alarm us, but can instead amuse us. However, when infidelity or other kinds of sexual inappropriateness becomes the subject of human behavior, we are no longer amused. More often than not those affected experience a shredding of souls and disruption of life.

Though troubling, sexual misconduct in the world is not surprising to any of us. But when it strikes within the Christian community, questions come to mind. Is he or she really a Christian? Surely such a blatant disregard for God's standards suggests a lack of commitment to the faith, doesn't it? Is the Holy Spirit alive and well in that person? How could he . . . ? How could she . . . ?

We know that Christians commit sexual sin. God's people are not immune to making stupid and destructive choices. But what I want to consider here is not whether we sin (of course we do), but whether we can be caught in the web of behaviors that seem out of our control. Can a Christian have an addiction? Can a person be a Christian and have a sexual addiction? The answer is yes to both questions. And when that addiction lies coiled and denied in the heart's left side, great hurt will occur.

Some of the most pernicious left-hearted lodgers are various kinds of addictions. For some, it is hard to believe that Christians can have addictions. Somehow it doesn't seem possible that the Spirit of God can live in the same soul environment with an addiction. But that choice to cohabit speaks of the grace of God toward us and His promise that He'll never leave us or forsake us, even if that means He'll have to muck about in our messes. We've been cleansed of the sin that separates us from God, but many of us have not been released from the bondage that continues to enslave us. That's what an addiction is: an enslavement. A more specific definition of addiction is to say that it is anything that consistently controls behavior regardless of negative consequences. We can be addicted to many things: alcohol, drugs, relationships, sex, even religion.

A Tragic Figure

Let me illustrate these statements through a brief study of the biblical character of Samson, who was, in my view, a tragically poignant fellow who didn't seem to have a clue about the left side of his heart. It would not have occurred to him that he had a sexual addiction. He was specifically called by God for a specific task, but he could not leave the women alone. His inability to rise to his calling ultimately cost him his life as well as his calling. He's a perfect example of a believer who didn't acknowledge the left side of his heart. Because of denial as well as resistance to spiritual truth, he died a tragic death.

Samson did not seem to recognize or question his left-leaning heart, which lusted after any woman who fueled his passions. It is interesting that the first recorded words we have from him were, "I have seen a Philistine woman . . ." (Judg. 14:2 NIV). Some time later, the biblical narrative reveals how totally enveloped Samson became in his yearning for yet another Philistine woman—a prostitute whom he sees sashaying about her hometown of Gaza. He wasted no time in yielding to his heart's left side, as Scripture states, "He went in to spend the night with her" (Judg. 16:1 NIV). Soon after the Gaza woman we are made aware of Samson's most destructive relationship yet with a woman named Delilah—also a prostitute, also a Philistine. But let's back up a bit and consider some history on Samson before we get into the Delilah debacle.

What is so mind-boggling about this womanizer is that Samson's conception was announced to his barren mother by an angel. The angel told her that she would have a son whom the Lord would use to deliver Israel from the tyranny of the Philistines. The angel also told the future mother that Samson would be a Nazirite. Ironically, Nazirites were under a special vow to God to restrain their carnal nature. This restraint would serve as a testimony to the Israelites that if they expected to receive God's blessing upon their lives, they must discipline themselves and determine to live morally.

For centuries the Philistines fought against Israel for the possession of Palestine, a portion of the Promised Land covenanted by God to Abraham and finally experienced through the leadership of Joshua. Isn't it interesting that they're still fighting for that property centuries later?

When Samson was born, the Israelites had been in bondage to the Philistines for forty years. Scripture states that Samson "grew and the LORD blessed him, and the Spirit of the LORD began to stir him . . ." (Judg. 13:24–25 NIV). Unfortunately, the Lord was not the only one who stirred him. For twenty years Samson led his people to numerous victories over the Philistines, but even so, he was continually preoccupied with his lustful passions. What a picture of a divided heart! On the right side is Samson's divine calling to deliver the Israelites to victory. Also on the right side is his awareness of God's particular covenant upon his life as a Nazirite to lead a morally exemplary lifestyle so as to experience God's unique blessing.

Perhaps like Dr. Jekyll, Samson reasoned he "could quit anytime" if he really put his mind to it. However, no amount of mind resistance or self-determination worked for Samson once he discovered the delicious Delilah.

Actually, Delilah was a setup because the Philistines knew Samson's weakness for women. They made a deal with Delilah: "The rulers of the Philistines went to her and said, 'See if you can lure him into showing you the secret of his great strength and how we can overpower him so we may tie him up and subdue him. Each one of us will give you eleven hundred shekels of silver'" (Judg. 16:5 NIV). Those were probably the best wages Delilah had ever been offered. She went to work immediately.

A part of Samson's Nazirite vow was that he was never to cut his hair. God used Samson's long hair as a vehicle through which He tangibly demonstrated His power. Three times Delilah attempted to learn the "secret of his great strength" so she could report to the Philistines how they could capture Samson, but each time Samson told her a different lie. Finally, "with such nagging she prodded him day after day until he was tired to death." We read in Judges 16:16–17 that he told her everything. "No razor has ever been used on my head . . . because I have been a Nazirite set apart to God since birth. If my head were shaved, my strength would leave me, and I would become as weak as any other man" (NIV).

Soon after this confession, Samson fell into a deep sleep in Delilah's lap. She sent word to the Philistines that Samson was ready for capture because she had cut off his hair, the source of his strength. "He awoke from his sleep and thought, 'I'll go out as before and shake myself free.' But he did not know that the LORD had left him" (v. 20 NIV).

Chilling words . . . the Lord had left him. The Philistines grabbed Samson, gouged out his eyes, put him in shackles, and set him to grinding grain in prison. Ironically, his eyes could never again be used to incite his passions.

However, Samson did have one last day of victory. That was the day the Philistines were having a drunken celebration honoring one of their pagan gods, Dagon, whom they thanked for delivering Samson into their hands. They called Samson from prison and set him up in their midst that they might taunt and ridicule him. "Now the temple was crowded with men and women; all the rulers of the Philistines were there, and on the roof were about three thousand men and women watching Samson perform" (Judg. 16:27 NIV).

What a great picture. This provides enough drama for a high-budget action movie! The scene as well as Samson's life concludes with this rich imagery:

> Then Samson prayed to the LORD, "O Sovereign LORD, remember me. O God, please strengthen me just once more, and let me with one blow get revenge on the Philistines for my two eyes." Then Samson reached toward the two central pillars on which the temple stood. Bracing himself against them, his right hand on the one and his left hand on the other, Samson said, "Let me die with the Philistines!" Then he pushed with all his might, and down came the temple on the rulers and all the people in it. Thus he killed many more when he died than while he lived. (Judg. 16:28–30 NIV)

You've got to admit there's something tremendously gratifying about the way God answered Samson's final prayer. In spite of Samson's continual capitulation to his flesh, his betrayal of his Nazirite vow, and his indifference to the call of God, God honored his last request.

Let me digress and consider Samson's mother. Can you imagine how she must have felt? She who was visited by an angel and told her son would be a deliverer for his people had to feel utterly confused and humiliated at the direction his life had gone. Someone could ask her at any time, "Where's Samson?" and she could respond with a degree of certainty, "Sleeping with the enemy."

We of course have no way of knowing how Samson's mother dealt with her feelings, but I imagine she anguished constantly over Samson's lack of fidelity and wondered at God's promise to her prior to Samson's birth. To all appearances, Samson could be seen as a spiritual failure who never rose to the calling placed upon his life in his mother's womb.

So what was Samson's problem? I suggested earlier that I believe he had a sexual addiction that he never faced and certainly never conquered. Remember, an addiction is defined as anything that consistently controls behavior regardless of negative consequences. Samson was totally controlled by his lust, and in spite of the threats to his safety and well-being, he persisted at all cost in satisfying his perceived need. When a person is powerless to resist a negative behavior in spite of tragic consequences, that person is probably enslaved to an addiction.

What should Samson have done? He should have faced the issue—confronted his left-hearted lodger head-on! But instead, he obviously felt there was nothing to face. In spite of godly parents who attempted to dissuade him from his patterns, Samson chose to ignore the dangerous consequences of his behavior until that behavior led to his death.

Owning the Problem

A number of years ago, a dear friend and colleague of mine was arrested for soliciting a prostitute not many miles from his home. This friend, whom I'll call John, is a highly educated Bible scholar with numerous published articles and books that continue to enrich my study. His arrest, which was detailed in the local paper, stunned me as well as broke my heart. It was later learned that this pattern of behavior had been going on for years, but he had just never been caught. In his letter of resignation were the poignant words "I just can't seem to stop myself."

Unlike Samson, John knew he had a problem, but for reasons I'm not privy to, he did not address it. As a result, his reputation, marriage, and ministry were seriously compromised.

Is it an oversimplification to say that if we will face, define, and cease to deny what exists on our heart's left side we can conquer something as destructive as sexual addiction? I do not believe it is an oversimplification at all. The reason I feel so dogmatically about that truth is that God wills for us wholeness as well as deliverance. But deliverance can't come until we "own" our problem. We can't hand something over to God until we've handed it to ourselves through admitting its existence.

We, as an embarrassed nation, watched Bill Clinton go through the denial process about his sexual addiction. Denying emphatically that he was guilty of wrongdoing, he insisted instead that he was the victim of a right-wing conspiracy group. He staunchly maintained his innocence until DNA results proved otherwise. His reluctant admission of wrongdoing came only after he had tried all other dishonest avenues. Proverbs 28:13 states, "You can't whitewash your sins and get by with it; you find mercy by admitting and leaving them" (MSG).

Not only must we face the issue and stop denying it, we must take personal responsibility for our behavior. Often we hear excuses such as, "I can't help it . . . I had a dysfunctional family" or more specifically, "I can't help it . . . I was abused as a child." Those reasons have been labeled the "abuse excuse." Certainly abuse usually sets up patterns of behavior that work against healthy living patterns. But by taking responsibility for behavior that works against us and threatens to destroy us, we can say instead, "I was abused . . . I had a dysfunctional family . . . But I am working hard to reverse those patterns that were put into place at an early age. I recognize the destructiveness of such behavior and by God's grace and with His enablement, I refuse to be victimized by my background!"

Several days ago, I asked a friend whom I will call Gail to read this chapter from the perspective of her own experience. Her father, no longer living, had been fired from the administrative hierarchy of his church denomination for repeated and inappropriate sexual behavior. His termination was a highly publicized event and, of course, devastating as well as humiliating to the family. Gail was fourteen years old when this occurred and had always adored her dad. She told me he was a gentle, thoughtful father who had listened to her young heart with great sensitivity. When he died a year later, she felt she had lost her best friend as well as a loving father.

She continues to be mystified about the reasons for her father's behavior but wanted me to underscore the value of the church's coming alongside the "wounded ones." Her church community provided compassion, grace, and love to her dad, to Gail, and to her mom in ways that are indelibly etched in Gail's heart and for which she will always be grateful. Her enormous regret is that her father didn't seek help for a pattern he must have known was destructive and for which he would one day pay a gigantic price.

However, there is comfort for Gail, not only in the memory of her dad's kindness to her and the church community's graciousness to the family, but also in a passage of Scripture highlighted in her dad's Bible. In this particular scripture Gail assumes her father sought refuge and comfort:

> In you, O LORD, I have taken refuge;
> let me never be put to shame.
> Rescue me and deliver me in your righteousness;
> turn your ear to me and save me.
> Be my rock of refuge,
> to which I can always go;
> give the command to save me,
> for you are my rock and my fortress. (Ps. 71:1–3 NIV)

Unfortunately, the comfort Gail's dad found in Scripture was not enough to change the tragic course of his life. "If only Dad had had the courage to seek help," Gail said, "maybe he'd be alive today."

Getting Help

God does promise to be a refuge and to save us, but I'm convinced that one of the ways He does that is to use practical and human means to accomplish our healing. Just as I would hotfoot it to a dentist for a toothache or to a doctor for strep throat, I need to seek help from professionals for an addiction.

The March 2001 issue of *Christianity Today* featured an article on the degree of Internet pornography addiction among Christians. Focusing specifically on the double life of a youth pastor who ultimately got caught, the article stated that pornography use is on the rise and the number of pastors becoming entangled in pornography on the Web is growing.[1]

Psychologists suggest that because of on-line porn's accessibility, anonymity, and affordability, a pastor who would never visit an adult bookstore or rent explicit videos can download images in the privacy of his or her home or office. Perhaps the pressure to lead an exemplary moral life, the intense on-the-job emotional stress, and a lack of peer accountability contributes to the risk of pornography abuse and addiction among Christians in full-time ministry. Harry Schaumburg, director of Stone Gate Resources, a counseling retreat center in Colorado for Christian leaders struggling with sexual addiction, believes "cybersex" seems to temporarily fill a void in their lives. About half the clients Schaumburg treats are pastors who feel pressured and isolated. They experience a sense of intimacy through porn use even though they know it to be a false intimacy.

Admitting that you are caught in the clutches of addiction is the first step to recovery. Seeking help outside yourself is the second step. Understandably, most addicts don't seek help until forced to do so because their shame is great and the addiction gripping. But I am heartened by the availability of support for those who dare to step out for "rescue" and seek the fulfillment of God's promise to be a rock and a fortress.

I am indebted to the research of *Christianity Today* for the following resources that offer Christ-centered help for those struggling with Internet pornography and sexual addiction. This list is meant to be a service to readers and not necessarily an endorsement.

CHRISTIAN COUNSELING CENTERS

Barnabus Christian Counseling Network
www.barnabus.com

This association of Christian counselors provides on-line counseling.

Esther Ministries
www.estheronline.org
877.6.ESTHER
P.O. Box 2874
Tupelo, MS 38803

Especially for spouses of sex addicts, this ministry offers regional counseling workshops.

Psychological Counseling Services
www.pcsearle.com
480.947.5739
7530 East Angus Drive
Scottsdale, AZ 85251

This Christian counseling center specializes in intensive outpatient therapy, including treatment and restoration for clergy couples through its New Hope Education Foundation.

Pure Life Ministries
www.purelifeministries.org
859.824.4444
P.O. Box 410
Dry Ridge, KY 41035

Founded by a former sex addict and his wife, this ministry offers live-in treatment programs of six to twelve months.

Stone Gate Resources
www.stonegateresources.com
303.688.5680
11509 Palmer Divide Road
Larkspur, CO 80118

Through its Restoration Project, this ministry provides counseling for pastors and their congregations. Ten-day, on-site brief intensive counseling sessions also are available for individuals, couples, and families.

REFERRALS AND INFORMATION

National Association for Christian Recovery
www.christianrecovery.com
714.529.6227
P.O. Box 215
Brea, CA 92822-0215

This ministry offers counseling referrals and resources for leading recovery support groups.

Pure Intimacy
www.pureintimacy.org
719.531.3400, Ext. 2700
(Focus on the Family Counseling Referral Line)
877.233.4455
(Focus on the Family Pastoral Care Line)

This ministry includes counseling referrals and resources for Web porn addicts and spouses.

Victims of Pornography
www.victimsofpornography.org

May is Victims of Pornography month. This Web site includes re-source lists and information to raise awareness of the issue.

Addiction has the power to destroy, but God has the power to deliver. In the story of Samson and his ultimate plea to God to grant his last sightless request, we see God's grace and mercy as He heard and answered Samson's prayer. It's never too late to plead with God, no matter how blind you have been about the destructive, addictive patterns in your life. No matter how tight the hold an addiction has on you or on someone you love, it is God's desire and intention to enable, deliver, and heal.

Chat Room Possibilities

1. Do you believe that it is possible to be a Christian and still have addictions? Why do you believe as you do?

2. Why do you suppose God chose to have a special call on Samson's life when Samson appeared to be disobedient to that call? Do you know any other "Samson types"? Did God make an error in judgment in setting Samson apart as a Nazirite?

3. What is meant by "owning the problem"? Why is "ownership" so crucial to success? What is your experience in the ownership process?

4. Do you think there are Christians (like Samson) who never seem to get victory and release from their addictions? If so, how do you explain that?

5. Do you agree that "it's never too late"? What is your experience with that concept?

I'd Rather Discuss Neckties

TALKING ABOUT THE *M* WORD

I have deliberated for several weeks about the wisdom of writing on the subject of this chapter. Once deciding I should, I wrote it and then deliberated over it with my editors. Should it be included in this book? Is the topic pertinent in view of the larger issues addressed? Will readers be offended? Will it be instructive, helpful, and hopefully shame-eliminating; or will it be a source of contention, criticism, and defeat the purpose altogether?

The reason I decided to take the risk is that so frequently this topic came up in therapy sessions for both men and women. Questions like, "Is it a sin? I've always been taught it was shameful, bad, and a disgusting practice . . . is it? What does the Bible say about it?"

Because there is such shame associated with it and because shame is such a toxic tenant, perhaps a candid and biblical examination of this topic will be beneficial in spite of the potential discomfort it may produce.

When I told one of my friends the subject of this chapter, she stopped dead in her tracks and said, "Well, surely you're not going to write the word, are you?"

"Well, yes," I answered. "How else can I discuss it?"

"Why do you have to discuss the word or even mention the word, Marilyn? For that matter, why do you have to write about it at all? Who wants to read about it anyway?"

Because the subject put her in a tiny huff, I switched the conversation to a different topic—discussing the ridiculousness of men's neckties. Her question was, "How could you trust a person who would go about his day wearing a little noose around his neck?"

The shame-producing, unprintable word my friend and I were starting to discuss and the one about which I felt hesitation to write is *masturbation*. Now, if that word causes your mouth to freeze in a straight line or sets off a pronounced facial tic I could use the euphemism "self-pleasure," which is popular in psychiatrist circles. I personally find that phrase sufficiently ill-defined as to include pleasures like the consumption of milk chocolate, the smell of fresh bread, or my Bose CD speakers. Perhaps I should refer to it as the *M* word.

But before we select our term, let me digress for a touch of historical trivia on this delicate subject, which I must admit gives me a giggle (the trivia, not the subject). Over the centuries social critics have almost unanimously proclaimed masturbation as the vilest behavior known to mankind. Dr. William Alcott, founder of the American Physiological Society, described in *A Young Man's Guide* (1840) how masturbation makes a man tottering, wrinkling, and hoary. (I had to look up the meaning of *hoary*. It means covered with gray hair . . . oops!) It leads inevitably to insanity, Saint Vitus's dance, epilepsy, blindness, apoplexy, hypochondria, consumption, and a sensation of ants crawling from the head down to the spine. And Dr. Alcott (uncle to Louisa May Alcott) goes on to advise that unless the abominable practice is abandoned, death is inevitable!

In the 1800s, jewelers designed miniature handcuffs to restrain children from indulging themselves. There was also an adolescent boy's equivalent of the chastity belt: a small wire cage that locked over the genitals. The father was instructed to keep the key on his person at all times. If the beleaguered child thought there might be some relief when he went to bed, J. L. Milton described an invention guaranteed to work when self-discipline didn't. Writing in the twelfth edition of *Spermatorrhea*, published in 1887, Milton described the device that, when clipped to the child's bedsheets, rang an alarm in the parents' room if the boy had an erection.

It is obvious then that the subject and practice of masturbation has a reputation for shamefulness that dates back centuries. This is an unfortunate viewpoint because masturbation is not always shameful. We'll discuss instances when it is unhealthy and we'll also discuss instances when it is not. But in order for us as conscientious Christians to feel secure in removing the shame label attached to this activity, we need to look to Scripture to be sure we're on solid ground.

Biblical Guidelines

Historically a number of biblical passages have been used to condemn masturbation. However, virtually all current biblical expositors believe those passages have nothing to do with masturbation. But to be on the safe side, let's review these passages.

The first two are Leviticus 15:16 and Deuteronomy 23:9–11. Moses is writing about behavior that is acceptable in the camp. The Leviticus verse reads, "Now if a man has a seminal emission, he shall bathe all his body in water and be unclean until evening" (NASB). The Deuteronomy passage states, "When you go out as an army against your enemies, then you shall keep yourself from every evil thing. If there is among you any man who is unclean because of a nocturnal emission, then he must go outside the camp; he may not reenter the camp. But it shall be when evening approaches, he shall bathe himself with water, and at sundown he may reenter the camp" (NASB).

When expositors first interpreted those passages, the references to a man's "wet dream" were thought of as reference to masturbation. It is common knowledge now that wet dreams occur without being brought on by masturbation. Wet dreams are simply the way the body eliminates the buildup of seminal fluids. They are automatic responses that cannot be controlled.

In looking at the whole context of the passages, it is clear that Moses was thinking of nocturnal emission as a natural body function because he deals with other emissions from the body that occur for both men and women, including the women's menstrual cycle. If we assume those passages are condemning masturbation, then we would have to conclude that menstruation is also condemned.

The primary passage used to condemn masturbation is the story of Onan found in Genesis 38:8–10. It reads:

Then Judah said to Onan, "Go in to your brother's wife, and perform your duty as a brother-in-law to her, and raise up offspring for your brother." And Onan knew that the offspring would not be his; so it came about that when he went in to his brother's wife, he wasted his seed on the ground, in order not to give offspring to his brother. But what he did was displeasing in the sight of the LORD; so He took his life also. (NASB)

Peculiar as this anecdote sounds, we need to put the passage in context and understand the custom of the day. If a man died without an heir, it was the duty of his living brother to provide an heir for him by means of a sexual union with the widow. When the son was born, he would be considered the son of the dead brother rather than the son of the biological father. For some reason Onan did not want to support the custom as God's decree. He wanted to do things his way, so in the middle of the sexual experience with his brother's widow, he withdrew and ejaculated on the ground.

This passage has so frequently been used as a condemnation for masturbation that the act has sometimes been referred to as "Onanism." The reality, however, was that Onan was not self-stimulating; he was disobeying God's decree, and for that God punished him.

These three Old Testament passages most frequently used to condemn masturbation clearly provide no basis for that condemnation.

In the New Testament, 1 Thessalonians 4:3–4; Romans 1:24; and 1 Corinthians 6:9 were at one time used to condemn masturbation. All three of these passages are now understood to be references to homosexuality or immorality, not to self-stimulation. It appears safe then to conclude that the Bible does not deal directly with the subject of self-stimulation in either the Old or the New Testament. Any biblical guidelines we could bring to this subject would have to come about as an understanding of other principles taught in Scripture.

Dr. Archibald Hart, well-known Christian clinical psychologist, and his colleagues Dr. Catherine Hart Weber and Debra Taylor have written candidly and sensitively in their book *Secrets of Eve* about the sexuality issues women face. Concerning masturbation they state, "Now while we see no reason to view masturbation as a problem, please don't misunderstand us. We are not opening the door on unbridled masturbation."

They go on to say that there are, in their view, three conditions under which masturbation can be viewed as destructive and go against principles taught in Scripture: (1) when it is used to avoid sexual intimacy, (2) when it is used to fulfill an addictive urge, and (3) when it is used to foster lust or a desire for someone other than your partner.[1]

A Healthy Balance

Let's discuss now these three conditions. We first ask the question, "Does this practice interfere with my ability to express physical love to my spouse?" If it does, then obviously masturbation is taking from the healthy maintaining of sexual intimacy. On the other hand, if one partner desires a great deal of sexual activity and the other is less frequently interested, the couple might decide that self-stimulation is actually the most loving act the highly interested person can do since it does not put the spouse under pressure. There may be times when abstinence from sexual relations is necessary. In those circumstances perhaps the most loving way to enjoy a sexual release will occur either by self-stimulation or by mutual stimulation. These occasions might be as a result of extensive periods of separate travel or illness. Also, there may be times of extreme outside pressure for one person, resulting in the preference to take care of his or her own sexual needs.

Having stated those justifications for self-stimulation, it is of course an unwise, possibly destructive activity if it is used to avoid sexual intimacy or to punish a spouse by satisfying oneself. In those instances there are emotional problems in the marriage that need to be addressed.

Another guideline for determining the appropriateness of self-stimulation is the matter of lust. The assumption most people make is that masturbation is always a lustful act. That is not necessarily so. Many people told me during various counseling sessions that they really didn't think of anyone as a sexual partner during those times of self-stimulation. They simply needed the release and found it not only pleasant, but beneficial.

Probably of greatest concern in terms of lustful masturbating activity is that associated with pornography. The common practice is to use pornography as a way of experiencing stimulation and masturbation as a release for that stimulation. This behavior can become addictive as well as a means of isolating from the marital partner. Once again this signals problems in the marriage. The point to be made, however, is that all self-stimulation is not necessarily lustful.

Another concern is when masturbation is used to fulfill an addictive urge. Very frequently adults who self-stimulate addictively are those for whom inappropriate touching and stimulating occurred as a child. A client of mine was relieved to realize that her addictive masturbation could be traced to her nanny who had cared for her during infancy. My client's parents were missionaries in India, and it was customary for nannies to use genital stimulation as a means of inducing sleep for the babies in their charge. This was not considered perverted or questionable in that culture, but merely practical. However it did set up an early sexual awakening in my client that was troublesome.

It is also common for young incest victims to self-stimulate addictively. This kind of compulsivity reflects issues that need to be addressed. Remember, one of the functions of addiction is to distract a person from life issues that need to be acknowledged and dealt with. If masturbation becomes one of those distractions, then it is unhealthy as well as unwise.

The sexual drive in all human beings is a natural, God-given urge. It gets out of balance and becomes no longer natural if one becomes mastered or enslaved by it. This drive is not to be fulfilled at the expense of those we love. Though masturbation relieves physical need, sex is about far more than physical release. It is about a symbolic union of two people united in marriage for whom love is tenderly expressed. That union was instituted by God Himself and is a holy sanctioning of the relationship.

But for those who are single, without the benefit of a marriage partner, the issue of self-stimulation becomes one of discreet and balanced caring for the self. That caring can be pure as well as fulfilling. The guideline to be followed is to remember that we are the temple of the Holy Spirit. It is not the urge that defiles the temple, but how that urge is expressed.

If masturbation is a secret stalking about your heart's left side, reeking of shame, consider the concerns discussed in this chapter. Are you addicted? Do you use it as an escape from marital intimacy? Is your mind lustfully focused upon specific persons? If so, those responses indicate some issues exist for you that would benefit from a gentle inquiry with a professional, from books, or from time with a trusted friend. But the shame label is inappropriate because the essence of you is who you are and not what you do. Who you are is one loved, cleansed, and forgiven by your Father. Your secret does not deserve to wear those bright red letters; He removed them when you became His child.

Chat Room Possibilities

1. Why do you think this subject produces so much discomfort and even shame?

2. Do you think it's unrealistic to say lust is not always a component with masturbation?

3. When did you first learn about masturbation?

4. Do you consider masturbation a shameful act . . . a sin?

5. Is this a topic parents should talk about with their children? If so, how should that "educational chat" proceed? What should be taught?

Just Get Over It

COPING WITH SEXUAL ABUSE

I'd like to tell you a story found in 2 Samuel 13:1–22 that puts my teeth into high grind. King David (of Bathsheba fame) had a son named Amnon, who fell madly in love with his half sister Tamar. Because she was a virgin princess, Tamar, according to Jewish custom, lived in strict seclusion. That created a problem for Amnon because he could never be with her in spite of their brother-sister status. However, his desire for access to her was based solely on lust and not brotherly love.

Tamar was gorgeous, innocent, tender, and compassionate. Amnon became so lovesick that Jonadab, their cousin, asked Amnon what in the world was wrong with him. He looked "haggard morning after morning." When Amnon confessed his hopeless love for Tamar, Jonadab's scheming and wicked mind went into full throttle; he came up with a plan. The plan was for Amnon to pretend to be sick, which would provoke a visit from his father, King David. Amnon would ask his father if

Tamar could come to him and prepare a meal in his private residence. According to plan, the king agreed and sent word to Tamar at the palace instructing her to come to Amnon's house and prepare his food. Obediently she rushed to her brother's residence.

"Then Amnon said to Tamar, 'Bring the food here into my bedroom so I may eat from your hand.' And Tamar took the bread she had prepared and brought it to her brother Amnon in his bedroom. But when she took it to him to eat, he grabbed her and said, 'Come to bed with me, my sister'" (vv. 10–11 NIV).

She cried out in protest that, should she do such a wicked thing, it would be a disgrace to both of them. She even pleaded that if he was so determined to have her, "Please speak to the king; he will not keep me from being married to you." But he refused to listen to her and "since he was stronger than she, he raped her."

"Then Amnon hated her with intense hatred. In fact, he hated her more than he had loved her." Amnon said to her, "Get up and get out!" She begged him not to send her away because, "sending me away would be a greater wrong than what you have already done to me." (According to Mosaic Law, if a man meets a virgin who is not pledged to be married and he rapes her, he must marry the girl because she has been violated. The Israelite custom was that if he did not marry her, she then had to remain unmarried for the rest of her life.)

When Absalom, Tamar's full brother, learned about the rape of his sister, he said, "'Be quiet now, my sister; he is your brother. Don't take this thing to heart.' And Tamar lived in her brother Absalom's house a desolate woman." We read further that "when King David heard all this, he was furious." But in spite of his being furious, he did nothing. He neither rebuked nor disciplined Amnon. Two years later, Absalom murdered Amnon "because he had disgraced his sister Tamar."

This account of betrayal by trusted family members is as current in its themes as if it appeared in last week's *People* magazine. There is the parent who knows but does nothing, the brother who abuses and gets away with it, the cousin who participates by setting up the victim, and the other brother who says in essence, "Don't make a big deal of this; after all it's only your brother. Just get over it." As is so often the case with incest or rape, there is no advocate for the victim. Tamar lived in shame the rest of her life.

Was shame an appropriate emotion for Tamar to feel? What did she do to deserve it? Was not her innocence utterly betrayed by all those who should have protected her? Where was justice for her? Did she ever receive justice? Did the fact that Absalom murdered the perpetrator give her peace or remove her from the poison societal custom imposed upon her? Did that murder perhaps serve as justice for her? The answers to these questions are no, nothing, yes, none, no, no, and no!

I have another question. Why do you suppose that incident was included in Scripture? Often the attitude of family members who are aware of sexual exploitation within the home are inclined to deny it or, like Absalom, say, "No big deal; forget it; get over it." God obviously does not view this crime in the same way Tamar's family members did! I believe God includes the story of Tamar to be an encouragement to those who have experienced sexual abuse. This innocent girl was heartlessly victimized and seemingly left alone without solace of any kind. God states over and over again that what concerns us also concerns Him. Psalm 56:8 assures us, "Thou hast taken account of my wanderings; put my tears in Thy bottle; are they not in Thy book?" (NASB). God saw the injustice done to Tamar and it grieved Him. I believe He wants us to know His stand on that issue.

A Cry for Justice

Interestingly enough, Isaiah 1:17 reads, "Seek justice, reprove the ruthless; defend the orphan, plead for the widow" (NASB). God is not passive about injustice. I believe He would encourage anyone who has been sexually victimized not to sink into passivity and denial, but to "seek justice." What does that mean? Do we kill the offender as Absalom did? Romans 12:17, 19 instructs us to "Never pay back evil for evil to anyone. . . . Never take your own revenge, beloved, but leave room for the wrath of God, for it is written, 'Vengeance is Mine, I will repay,' says the Lord" (NASB).

Then how do we seek justice? We seek justice by resurrecting the soul that was murdered. Soul murder is what happens when one's personal dignity, self-esteem, and ability to feel joy, express pleasure, receive love, or extend love have been choked into lifeless oblivion. Is resurrection from all that possible? Absolutely. Why am I so dogmatic on this fact? Because God wills wholeness for the soul and healing for the spirit, and His own resurrection from death to life breathed possibility into both.

Let me give you a very personal illustration of God's resurrection power ultimately infusing a murdered soul. After our daughter Beth's graduation from high school, she waitressed at a restaurant near our home. She wanted to earn some extra money prior to leaving in the fall for Westmont College.

There was a waiter there from a foreign country whose culture is not known to value women but who appeared to Beth to be winsome, gentle, and kind. She was drawn to his stories of anguish about his politically imprisoned brothers, the murder of his father, and the terror of his mother—all living in the homeland from which this young man had escaped. Beth has always had a heart for the disenfranchised people of the world and feels personally called to help in some way. (In the third grade she took a little boy in her class under her wing because he was poor, had bad clothes, and smoked. She felt we should adopt him because his father was in jail and his mother was an alcoholic. However, when he repeatedly stole her lunch money and then lied about it, she became disillusioned about his potential for rehabilitation.)

Ken and I were ill at ease over the developing relationship between Beth and the waiter. He was in his late twenties, and Beth was not yet eighteen. We felt the need not to be judgmental and yet also felt parental concern. When the waiter asked if she would go out with him one night after work, we told Beth that we did not have peace about it and that she could not go. Beth viewed us as narrow-minded and lacking in compassion. Unbeknownst to us, she went anyway. At the conclusion of the evening, he raped her.

Beth had been extremely principled throughout high school and felt strongly about protecting her virginity. She was one of the very few in her graduating class who did. That this highly protected part of her being was wrenched from her was devastating. She was innocent and sought only to be a solace to one whose life circumstances seemed so brutal. He extended that brutality to include her.

Like Absalom, Beth's brother, Jeff, wanted to murder the guy—or at least maim him badly. But he disappeared. He had raped a minor and was working without a green card. He got away with it all. Beth was left in her desolation.

For years Beth struggled with periodic bouts of depression. She felt her kindness had been betrayed and that God had not protected her. She had gone contrary to her parents' direction, but the questions in her mind were, Did my punishment have to be so severe? What about those years of purposed sexual fidelity? Did that not count for something in God's eyes?

It has taken time, therapy, and a renewed trust in the God who sees sin and grieves over it to resurrect Beth's soul. But she is now the mother of two darling little boys, Ian and Alec, and she works as a counselor/social worker for a school district. Ironically the position she holds as a counselor is for the severely disenfranchised and impoverished population of the district. It is a program her father as school superintendent introduced to the local community long before he died and long before Beth and her family moved here. Little did Ken imagine the very program he initiated would one day hire his daughter to further his goals.

The Secret Crime

One of the most heartbreaking secrets festering to the left of the heart's zipper is incest. Many women (estimates run as high as 50 percent) do not remember their childhood incestuous experiences until something triggers the memory in adulthood. They were told, "Just get over it," so memory buried it, where hopefully it would remain unnoticed and undetected.

For the remainder of this chapter I'd like to deal with the subject of incest and its effects upon the soul. I'd like to suggest that if you are uncomfortable with the topic, if you feel nervous, fearful, or unsafe, please skip this chapter and move to the next one. If perchance you think you may have issues about sexual exploitation but are not sure, it's important for you to know that this is a topic that requires sensitive timing. The operative phrase is "when you're ready." If you are not ready, you are not being a wimp; you are showing sensitivity to yourself, which you highly deserve.

If indeed more than 50 percent of female incest survivors do not remember their incest, what's the point of dredging it up? Because any assault to the soul, any murderous behavior that takes the life of the soul, is slated for rebirth . . . resurrection. Though the memories may not be immediately retrievable, the behavior of the victim inevitably reflects the soul murder that has occurred. When we understand the origins of some of those behaviors, we are apt to be more sensitive about what has kicked that behavior into place.

For instance, during childhood, experiences of incest interfere with the development of high self-esteem and a healthy self-concept. The effects of the trauma and fear can lead to chronic depression, guilt, and a sense of powerlessness. Often these feelings play out in a number of self-destructive activities in adulthood, such as alcoholism, drug abuse, suicide attempts, and sexual relationships in which the woman continues to be victimized by men who physically mistreat her and demean her.

An incest survivor learns not to expect reciprocity in a relationship.

Because she was expected to meet the needs of her perpetrator to the neglect of her own, she learns that others don't really care about her inner concerns, so neither should she.

The self-concept of an incest victim is especially damaged because the victim doubts her own perceptions of reality. Children gain self-esteem by learning to trust their own feelings and experiences and by receiving affirmation about those feelings from others. When those feelings and experiences are not validated, but are instead discounted, the child chooses to believe the adult even though that adult may be the perpetrator. To doubt a parent's honesty is devastating to the child because she depends on the adult for an understanding of the world.

Beth told me yesterday of an especially heartbreaking family she is working with. A ten-year-old girl is causing continual disruptions in class and provoking fights on the playground. As Beth has worked to uncover the various family dynamics in the child's home, she learned the little girl is fondled sexually every night by her mother's boyfriend and forced to sleep with him while her mother works the night shift at a truck stop restaurant. He has recently forced sexual penetration. When Beth told her that was wrong and that the boyfriend had no right to touch her, that her body belonged to her and no one else, the little girl was stunned. She had been fondled by stepfathers, uncles, and brothers for as long as she could remember. That she had rights was beyond her comprehension.

As this child comes into her teen years, she may predictably gravitate toward one of two extreme sexual lifestyles. She may become socially and sexually withdrawn or she may plunge into a stage of promiscuity and sometimes self-destructive sexual activity.

The withdrawal response can reflect her fears about sex, anxieties about partners, and poor self-image. Symptoms of withdrawal include refusing dates, staying socially isolated, pretending that sex does not exist, and denying sexual feelings. She may imagine that dating will require sexual willingness and responsiveness. She may believe her date's main focus will be getting sex. Sexual abuse survivors have little trust in their own ability to say no or to protect themselves. To this child the right to say no is foreign.

The other potential lifestyle is to enter into frequent sexual activity, which can be a form of self-destructive punishment. The victim may feel guilty for the incest and self-degrading activities. She tells herself, *This is all I'm good for anyway.* Studies have shown that a high percentage of prostitutes were sexually abused in childhood.

Beth's little fifth grader is already dressing very provocatively and, because she's a gorgeous child, inviting a lot of sexual attention from older boys. It appears to Beth the child will fall into the category of early and frequent promiscuity.

Sexual abuse is not only a secret, it is a secret crime; rarely are there witnesses. Studies reveal that shame and secrecy keep a child from talking to siblings about the abuse even if all the children in the family are being sexually abused. In contrast, if a child is physically or emotionally abused, that abuse is likely to occur in front of the other children in the family.

Because sexual abuse is a secret, it has a tremendous impact on the family even though that impact may be hidden from the outside world. Family members may or may not be consciously aware of the abuse, but even if they do know about it, they do not speak of it. Oddly enough, everyone knows when to disappear, what not to question, and when to look away. Because Beth's student has ceased to look away and decided to speak out, the family cover has been blown. Child Protective Services is now involved and hopefully will be a protective benefactor. Nonetheless, deep damage has already occurred, not only to Beth's student, but also, not surprisingly, to her two older sisters.

Finding Healing

So what do you do now if you suspect that your soul has been deeply damaged by sexual exploitation? To begin with, you decide that no matter what, you want to find healing for your soul. God is the healer. It is He and He alone who strengthens us for this journey, and He and He alone takes the shards of our splintered souls and lovingly puts them together again. Place yourself in His gentle custody. Trust Him for your first step and those that will follow.

Just as God uses dentists, doctors, and others in various helping professions, He also uses therapists. My suggestion for you now is to begin the search for a therapist who specializes in treating victims of sexual abuse. I realize many survivors and partners of survivors feel anxious about seeking professional help. Picking up the phone to call a therapist is sometimes the toughest step in the entire process. That makes sense because incest and sexuality are both very personal areas that have been shrouded in secrecy for eons. This may be especially true for Christians who more typically avoid discussion about sexual experiences. There are feelings of shame, embarrassment, and fear of what others think that often inhibit people from seeking help. Because of the fact that sexual exploitation (incest and rape) results in the betrayal of trust, trust is inevitably an issue in therapy. Survivors have learned they cannot afford to trust blindly; the cost has been too great. This being the case, acknowledge the fact that trusting people is not easy for you and be as deliberate as you need to be in selecting a therapist.

A sensible way to start your therapist search is to talk to your pastor, priest, or other spiritual caregiver. Also, consider talking to your family doctor, a gynecologist, a mental health referral service, an incest treatment program, a women's resource agency, a rape crisis center, a psychologists association, a sex therapists association, and friends who may be able to supply the names of persons they know to have good reputations. Identify the therapists who are recommended by more than one source. Call them and ask questions.

While interviewing therapists either on the phone or in person, you may want to ask questions such as: What experience and training do they have in treating incest and sexuality issues? Are they fully licensed?

How would they describe their style? What therapeutic methods do they use? What is their fee? Is the fee negotiable? Are they willing to have a short initial meeting free of charge? Trust your intuition; pick the therapist who sounds best and make an appointment.

It isn't necessary to be crazy about your therapist, but it is necessary to trust him or her. Feeling the respect, caring, and support from such a professional can be a powerful help as you start the healing process. If for some reason you feel strong negative feelings about one particular therapist, that is reason enough to eliminate that person from consideration.

As you begin your journey, remember that God walks your path with you. He knows the beginning from the end; there are no surprises to Him. He knows you have been a victim of a trauma that has had a profoundly negative effect upon you. He also knows you had no control over it or ability to escape from it. You are beautiful to Him, and He means to heal and restore you. Never, ever, does He say, "Just get over it."

Henri Nouwen reminds us of God's perspective in *The Road to Daybreak:* "I am your God . . . I see all of your actions. And I love you because you are beautiful, made in my own image. . . . Do not judge yourself. Do not condemn yourself. Do not reject yourself. . . . Come, come, let me wipe your tears, and let my mouth say . . . I love you, I love you, I love you."[1]

Chat Room Possibilities

1. Have you ever felt abandoned by God?

2. How do you answer the age-old question of why God allows bad things to happen to His people?

3. To what degree do you feel free to trust?

4. Do you feel the need to be "on guard" in your relationships?

5. How does your ability (or inability) to trust others affect your trust in God?

Part 3

Evicting Your
Toxic Tenants

14

Steps to Liberation

TAKING ACTION TOWARD WHOLENESS

Korean-born Paul Yonggi Cho is pastor of the largest church in the world. As his ministry was becoming international, Cho tried a little bargaining with God. He told God, "I will go anywhere You want me to go to preach the gospel of Jesus . . . I'll go anywhere, that is, except to Japan." Cho's animosity toward the Japanese was deep and unrelenting. He hated what the Japanese troops had done to the Korean people and to members of Cho's own family during World War II.

So guess what happened? God sent Cho to Japan with the specific assignment of preaching at a conference of one thousand Japanese pastors. Cho must have felt perfectly justified to do a few yeah buts with God. He may well have said, "Yeah, but God, You know I hate the Japanese. I don't want to bring the gospel to the Japanese . . . I resent them. Actually, I loathe them. Why would You ask me to do something I have no will or strength to do?"

Those yeah buts did not wear God down; Cho obediently went to Japan and the conference. When he was called upon to speak, he approached the podium, looked out over the Japanese audience, and the only words that came out of his mouth were, "I hate you; I hate you; I hate you." He slumped then over the pulpit, broke down, and began weeping uncontrollably. At least one, then two, then all one thousand pastors stood up. One by one they walked up to Cho, knelt at his feet, and asked forgiveness for what they and their people had done to him and to his people. Slowly but powerfully, God melted Cho's heart. Cho saw these broken and repentant Japanese pastors as his brothers in Christ. The Lord put a new message in his heart and then his mouth: "I love you; I love you; I love you."

When God told Jonah to go to Nineveh and warn the people they were doomed if they didn't repent and change their ways, Jonah did a huge yeah but. Jonah's unrecorded response could well have been, "Yeah, but God, those people are our enemies. Why should I care what happens to them? Quite frankly, I'd like to see them wiped out."

Jonah had perfectly good reasons not to want to go to Nineveh. Nineveh was the capital of Assyria. The Assyrians were a barbaric, cruel, bloodthirsty people who continually tyrannized the Israelites. Their specialty was to invade any city that looked good to them and steal the residents' stuff, rape their women, and claim their property. If the Assyrians didn't want the city, they merely set fire to it. They were a continual threat to the northern kingdom of Israel. The Assyrians were to Jonah what the Japanese were to Cho. Very simply, the Assyrians were not nice people.

What do we do about the behaviors of those "not nice" people who hurt us, deceive us, betray us, or even brutalize us? Surely we aren't expected to forgive them. Are there not some evils beyond forgiveness?

This agonizing question is the discussion point around which the powerful true story *The Sunflower* revolves. I'll briefly summarize it for you.

What Would You Have Done?

While in a concentration camp in Lemberg, Poland, the Jewish inmate Simon Wiesenthal and other prisoners were marched into town to work at various menial jobs in the hospital that housed wounded Nazi soldiers. One morning a nurse interrupted Wiesenthal's work, startling him with the command to follow her. She led him to the bedside of a dying S.S. officer. The man's head was swathed in bandages that were mottled with yellow pus stains and blood; there were holes for his eyes, mouth, and nose.

Karl, the dying soldier, was tortured by his conscience over what he had done to the Jews. He felt he could not die without being forgiven; he wanted forgiveness from a Jew. Simon was that random pick. Simon had no desire to hear the Nazi's confession, but he was afraid to resist, as he told in his gripping story. The officer began, "'I must tell you something dreadful . . . something inhuman.' Then his hand grasped mine. His fingers clutched mine tightly as though he sensed I was trying unconsciously to withdraw my hand. . . . 'I must tell you this horrible deed—tell you because you are a Jew.'" The confession began with the words "I was not born a murderer." With a mixture of horror and revulsion, anger and impotence, Simon was made to hear the innumerable injustices and atrocities perpetrated upon his people by this officer and his troops.

Concluding his confession, Karl struggled to sit up. "He put his hands together as if to pray. . . . I saw that he could not get the words past his lips. I was in no mood to help him. I kept silent." Again the officer begged for forgiveness that he might die in peace. In the "uncanny silence" that filled the room, Simon hesitated, looked again at Karl's folded hands, and wordlessly left the room. The soldier died later that day.

After this experience, on May 5, 1945, the American liberation occurred and Wiesenthal was a free man. He was free in body, but not totally free in his spirit. The image of the dying soldier, his pleading words for forgiveness, and Wiesenthal's refusal to grant it roiled in his mind. He decided to write out his experience and then draw us all into it with these soul-searching considerations:

> Was my silence at the bedside of the dying Nazi right or wrong? This is a profound moral question that challenges the conscience of the reader of this episode, just as much as it once challenged my heart and mind. There are those who can appreciate my dilemma, and so endorse my attitude, and there are others who will be ready to condemn me for refusing to ease the last moment of a repentant murderer.
>
> The crux of the matter is, of course, the question of forgiveness. Forgetting is something that time alone takes care of, but forgiveness is an act of volition, and only the sufferer is qualified to make the decision.
>
> You, who have read this sad and tragic episode in my life, can mentally change places with me and ask yourself the crucial question, "What would I have done?"[1]

Yes indeed . . . what would I have done? We in the Christian world are steeped in the theology that we must, at all cost to ourselves, forgive our enemies . . . those who hurt us. No matter how deeply or atrocious their deeds, we must forgive them.

One of my favorite writers and talk-show hosts is Dennis Prager. Prager, a Jew, suggests that there are times when forgiveness is a sin. It would be wrong to forgive. Prager wrote in the *Wall Street Journal* that forgiveness says that "no matter how much you hurt others, millions of your fellow citizens will forgive you. . . . Even by God, forgiveness is contingent upon the sincere repenting and it can be forgiven only by the one sinned against."

Many of you reading these words have been hurt by people who have never acknowledged what they did to you; neither have they asked for your forgiveness. Perhaps it is the husband who left you and your three children that he might "feel" once again—and he found that feeling he lost for you with another woman. He has not acknowledged his abandonment of you and the children; he has not asked forgiveness. Does Prager's logic provide you with a loophole not to forgive?

What about the trusted friend with whom you started a business? Through some maneuvering you did not anticipate, you find yourself not a part-owner after all. In fact, it now appears you will lose your investment as well as your business. Your "friend" hasn't even acknowledged what she did, and somehow it has been interpreted to others as your fault. Does your former friend deserve forgiveness?

When your husband, a sixth-grade teacher, was falsely accused of molesting a child in his classroom, he was fired. Upon further investigation it was learned that three disgruntled students had made up the story about one of them being molested. They were "curious to see what would happen." Apparently, it got out of hand and went further than they anticipated. In spite of being declared innocent after all, your husband was not reassigned to the classroom. The excuse: The parents are still a little jumpy after all the press coverage. Unforgivable?

The list could go on and on. As in all things, we look to Jesus and His Word for the final word on forgiveness. As you and I both know, He was very clear on the subject. Let's review.

The Interior Concentration Camp

The words found in the Lord's Prayer—"Forgive us our sins as we forgive those who trespass against us"—in essence say that if we don't forgive, we are not forgiven. Jesus underscores that thought in the parable of the unforgiving debtor. From that we are told that nothing anyone can do to us in life will ever be as bad as what we have done to God. We have rejected Him, ignored Him, disobeyed Him, and refused to honor Him. And yet, when we repent, He forgives us absolutely and continues to love us. Jesus, the object of horrifying and debasing human cruelty, said from the cross, "Father, forgive them, for they do not know what they are doing,"

Must we forgive even though forgiveness is not sought by the perpetrator of harm? Do we have to forgive even when the deed is unforgivable? Scripture says yes. The example of Jesus says yes. The Word of God says yes. "Yeah, but what if I don't want to? What if all the Scripture in the world will not motivate me to forgive? What if I simply do not have it in my heart even to try?"

Most of us, if we were to shine the light on the pileup to the zipper's left, would find a wad of resentment that has its root in an unforgiving spirit. Many of us would rather hang on to the resentment than forgive. We know forgiving will get rid of the resentment that is weighing us down, but even that is not sufficient motivation. The sobering truth about hanging on to the resentment is that we create for ourselves an interior concentration camp. In that camp we sit behind the bars of our anger, our resentment, our bitterness, and our refusal to "let them off the hook." We rationalize that stance by saying they don't deserve to be forgiven. What he did, she did, they did does not merit forgiveness . . . They went too far . . . The evil was too great . . . The damage was too deep.

Though "they" may not deserve forgiveness, may I suggest that neither do you deserve the consequences that come with a lack of forgiveness. It was bad enough to be hurt the first time, but it is inexcusable to find yourself imprisoned in the concentration camp for something you did not deserve.

Unforgiveness is like a lodger with leprosy. That leper cuddles up to other left-hearted lodgers, and together they give birth to ragings, addiction, depression, inability to trust, as well as myriad physical maladies. We can stay in the corner if we choose to, but God would rather there be a "Liberation Day" for each of us.

Forgiving those who do not deserve forgiveness does not mean that what they did was right. Forgiveness does not grant approval. Neither

182

does forgiveness grant them access to you and your life. Forgiveness simply sets *you* free from your self-imposed concentration camp. If you are to evict the lodgers, you must forgive and send the lodgers on their way. Without forgiveness, most of the lodgers won't budge. They don't need to; unforgiveness gives them permission to stay.

When God sent Paul Yonggi Cho to Japan, it was not to taunt him with his prejudice and hatred; it was to heal him of his prejudice and hatred. Cho was in a self-imposed concentration camp and didn't even know it. But God knew it, and He wanted Cho to be released . . . released to new light and inner healing.

"Mounting Up"

God wants that for us as well. If we truly want to evict the toxic tenants on our hearts' left side, we must first consider the unforgiveness that assures them of a home with us.

Are you willing to face any unforgiveness within you? If not . . . if you still simply don't feel it's possible to forgive, then are you willing to be made willing? If you can take just that step, God will meet you where you are. As you come to Him in prayer, admitting that you are not willing to forgive, but are willing to be made willing, you open yourself in obedience as Cho did. You allow God ultimately to melt your heart into one that no longer says, "I hate you." In His own time and in His own way, God's goal is that you may be able to say, "I love you."

As you are willing to be made willing, and as you attempt the eviction exercises in the following chapters, consider perhaps the most vivid illustration we have of how God meets us where we are: the biblical metaphor of the eagle. Scripture repeatedly compares us to eagles. What makes that comparison so apt is that the eagle, though the most powerful of all birds in creation, is utterly unable to launch itself into flight. All the flapping in the world will not get the eagle off the ground. It must catch a wind current in order to "mount up." In order to catch a current, the eagle spreads its wings in readiness *and waits*. Until the current comes, the eagle is powerless as well as earthbound. But once the wind does come, the bird soars freely, majestically, and powerfully.

What does this metaphor say to us? That we have access to the enabling currents of God. They and they alone are our empowerment. All the flapping, fretting, and fussing in the world will not get us airborne; we remain stuck in the morass of the left-hearted junk pile unless we choose to spread our wings. Then we wait for Him to lift us up and away from the toxicity in which we are stuck.

"They who wait for the LORD shall renew their strength, they shall mount up with wings like eagles" (Isa. 40:31). Until you are able to fly free, will you wait in readiness for the power of God to liberate you? He alone is our strength.

Chat Room Possibilities

1. How was forgiveness handled in your home? Was forgiveness given grudgingly, not at all, or freely? How have those early patterns shaped your current patterns?

2. Do you think it is humanly possible to fully forgive?

3. Are you aware of any health consequences you experience that may have their root in an unforgiving spirit? (These consequences can include backaches, headaches, high blood pressure, insomnia, irritable bowel syndrome, or colitis.)

4. Depression may also be a consequence of an unforgiving spirit. Do you see any link between the two in your life?

5. Why do you think forgiveness seems to be a priority for God?

15

Shame Busters

UNDERSTANDING
THE SOURCE OF SHAME

A year ago I finally yielded to the social pressure to buy a cell phone. I find cell phones exceedingly annoying, but one would of course be helpful in the event I'm ever stuck in Bisbee, Arizona; Fargo, North Dakota; or Maud, Texas. I suppose I would want to let someone know my location. Actually, I'm not sure who would be interested in knowing my whereabouts, but it is comforting to contemplate the possibility.

The fact that I'm technologically challenged was the major hindrance to purchasing a phone. However, my friend and technical consultant, Pat Wenger, explained how it worked, and I reluctantly became a cell phone owner.

Things were going moderately well until the word "edit" appeared inexplicably at the bottom of the screen several days after the purchase. No matter which button I selected, "edit" would not disappear. Now frankly, I've never felt warmly inclined toward that word. It conjures up images of a book editor's red-marking my manuscripts with the familiar criticism "too wordy." But the possibility that even my phone conversations might be subject to editing seemed utterly unreasonable.

Having punched every available button, I gave up editing "edit" and attempted to call my friend Luci. A male voice answered. That didn't fit. I said, "I'm sorry, I guess I punched in the wrong number." He pleasantly replied, "Don't be sorry" . . . long pause . . . then, "Mare Bear??" I responded, "Unco Neal??" It was my brother-in-law in Colorado!

I told him that I had a new phone that I had not yet mastered and that how I got him (he's an *A* for Atkinson and Luci's an *S* for Swindoll) was a mystery. Neil is well aware of my mechanical deficit and knew better than to try to figure it out with me. We had a wonderful visit and hung up. I didn't try to call Luci again . . . I figured Neil was too busy.

The next day, comforted by the mysterious disappearance of the word "edit," I decided to call Pat. Scrolling through the alphabet with the right-hand button, I punched in "Wenger" and waited. Nothing . . . no sound . . . nada. Holding the maddening little phone in the palm of my hand I walked over to my desk to see if the instruction booklet made any more sense than it had the day before. It didn't.

Muttering peevishly about the possibility of banishing my phone to live in solitary confinement with my two computers, I faintly heard my name. I was alone in the room. With deliberate enunciation I kept hearing, "Marilyn . . . Mar . . . i . . . lyn." I looked uncomprehendingly at my phone. The voice was coming from it. Putting the phone to my ear I tentatively said, "What?" It was Neil. He was laughing so hard he could barely talk. He was hearing my muffled mutterings and of course knew what had happened yet again. We had another pleasant conversation punctuated every now and then with guffaws of laughter (his, not mine).

Later in the day I decided to call Marge (Neil's wife and Ken's sister) to giggle together over my latest flash of technological genius. Thinking it'd be a cinch to call her since I'd connected with their number so effortlessly before, I punched "Atkinson." Pat Wenger answered.

My technical missteps add spice to my life and keep me on my toes. However, it is also true that I'm a bit embarrassed by myself. Small children click and mouse along effortlessly with their computers; the world chatters endlessly on cell phones, not one of which manages to connect with my brother-in-law in Colorado.

What's Marilyn's problem? Who exactly knows how to explain the faulty wiring in my brain that short-circuits my efforts to master technology? That frankly is not my concern! But in all seriousness, what is a concern is how I feel. Embarrassment has its root in shame. Though in this instance I have a light case of it, the fact that shame whispers demeaning messages in my ear when Neil answers instead of Pat has relevance for this chapter's emphasis.

Not one of us is exempt from the wide net of shame that envelops us to varying degrees at nearly all times. Any action that calls our competence into question produces shame. And as discussed throughout this book, shame inspires cover-ups, denial, and avoidance. We will do almost anything not to feel shame. Shame and its resulting behavior is kicked to the left of the zipper. Reminding ourselves of the shame influence, we come to the part of our discussion that will hopefully help us banish that shame pileup we keep talking about.

Exposing the Shame Root

To begin with, I'd suggest that almost all maladaptive behavior has its root in shame. That being the case, we need to know how to deal with that shame. Let's examine the issues we've described and run them through the shame grid just to assure ourselves that shame is the root cause of the left-hearted problems we've discussed.

Let's begin with lying. How does shame figure into lying? Most of the lies we tell are motivated by fear that the truth would not put us in a good light. We lie to prevent others from seeing or knowing the truth about us—a truth that exposes us as less than perfect. We are ashamed of being less than perfect; we think the lie preserves our image.

Similarly, when we present a false identity, we hope our mask will cause us to appear more acceptable, winsome, capable, worthy of praise, and lovable. Because shame messages convince us we are not lovable or capable, maybe a false ID will make up for the inherently inadequate person we perceive ourselves to be.

Anger is the result of not getting what we want when we want it. How does shame figure into anger? We want to be respected, loved, valued, and made to feel worthy of all we ask. If we don't get that, we'll frighten others into giving it by using anger. Why is there a need to command respect and love through anger? Usually because we didn't receive it in the early stages of development. Instead, we received just the opposite, which produced shame. We learned early on that anger got negative attention: At least we were not erased; at least we were noticed. We learned we could feel more powerful when we used our anger. And why do we need power? Because we're ashamed of our powerlessness, our inablilty to control the events of life and the responses of the people around us. Our effort to control heightens the anger response if the control is threatened.

The various addictions to which we become enslaved are distractions from the lack of value we attach to ourselves. We drink excessively so we don't feel. What emotion is being avoided? Shame. We don't want to feel or think that we're incapable of sustaining a relationship or performing well at a job. We drink because we don't want to feel and remember those childhood scenes of abuse that robbed us of our dignity and undermined our worth. Drinking addictively serves to distract us from the core-level feeling we have about ourselves. What is that feeling? That we are shameful, incapable human beings who have made a mess of life and who may be on the verge of being "found out."

What's the shame component in sexual addiction? Once again the

190

sexual acting out distracts from the real pain and hurt the addict does not want to face. What is that real pain? Shame. The shamed person cannot bear to hear the inner tapes that play on and on and on. Staying busy and distracting the self through addictive behavior will work until a new barrage of shame messages based on the current behavior starts to clamor.

If we can recognize the shame root that exists in each of us, then we have a starting place for understanding, healing, and ultimately evicting the toxic tenants that rob us of abundant life. Henri Nouwen writes in *Life of the Beloved*:

> I have come to realize that the greatest trap in our life is not success, popularity or power, but self-rejection. . . . When we have come to believe in the voices that call us worthless and unlovable, then success, popularity and power are easily perceived as attractive solutions. The real trap, however, is self-rejection. I am constantly surprised at how quickly I give in to this temptation. As soon as someone accuses me or criticizes me, I am rejected, left alone or abandoned, I find myself thinking: "Well, that proves once again that I am a nobody." Instead of taking a critical look at the circumstances or trying to understand my own and others' limitations, I tend to blame myself—not just for what I did, but for who I am. My dark side says: "I am no good . . . I deserve to be pushed aside, forgotten, rejected and abandoned."[1]

Reprogramming

Self-rejection is the core component of shame. However those messages got taped in the brain, it is never too late to reverse them. Those messages can be retaped by choosing to say, "I love myself." That message is not arrogant, egotistical, or self-aggrandizing. Rather, that message profoundly agrees with the words we receive about ourselves from God. In fact, He is almost a broken record on that subject. To fully agree with God's assessment of us will serve as a shame buster and radically change our lives.

So here's the first step in dealing with the shame pileup: Determine to love yourself unconditionally. No matter whom you perceive yourself to be, say to yourself over and over again, "I love you." As you're driving to work, washing your hair, getting the car serviced, cooking, cleaning, bathing, e-mailing, etc., repeatedly say your God-approved, God-endorsed message, "I love you."

If that message sticks in your throat, you must remember that in loving ourselves unconditionally as God does, we love and accept ourselves based, not on what we do, but on who we are. There's the tough part. Many of us feel we can perhaps love ourselves if we do something well, if our performance is good. Maybe then we deserve being loved. But how can we love ourselves when we make mistakes and do embarrassing things? That's the whole point; that's the shame-buster element. Poor performance has historically produced a shame response. If we love ourselves unconditionally, then even when we blow it badly, making huge or small mistakes, we do not waver in our agreement with God that we are still lovable—because He says we are!

I'm certainly not suggesting we ignore our mistakes and refuse to take responsibility for them. Our mistakes can present vital opportunities to learn about ourselves and what God would have us do differently. Mistakes are opportunities for feedback; we learn what works and what doesn't work.

While we learn to practice our "game," we continue to love ourselves no matter how many golf balls we send crashing through the windows of the house located too close to the sixth tee. By refusing to cater any longer to the shame messages that drive us, we bust out of our interior prison and discover what we are created for: life . . . abundant life.

Chat Room Possibilities

1. Do you agree that shame is the root of most of our maladaptive patterns? Why or why not?

2. As you look at the hurting areas of your life, can you identify the role that shame plays? Can you trace that shame to its original source?

3. Why is it so hard to truly receive God's unconditional love for us? What keeps us from accepting that message?

4. Who, in your human experience, has loved you unconditionally?

5. Is it possible for human beings to love unconditionally? How is this accomplished or why is it not accomplished?

16

Dead and Buried

PUTTING OUR SINS AWAY

William Faulkner's brilliant short story "A Rose for Emily" is one of the most startling as well as morbidly arresting stories ever written. (In spite of his fake war injuries, alcoholism, and inability to sustain intimate relationships, Faulkner was one of America's finest writers.) The narrative of this short story revolves around a love experience of Miss Emily Grierson and its effect upon her behavior and upon the people in the town of which Miss Emily is the last of a dying, southern aristocracy. (Before I launch into the telling of this story, I should probably warn you it is not for the faint of heart. It has something to say to us, though, so I hope you'll hang in there with me.)

When the flamboyant, "not-the-marrying-kind-of-guy" Homer Barron came to town as the foreman of a construction company contracted for the paving of the town's sidewalks, the townspeople were surprised to see Miss Emily on Sunday afternoon driving with Homer in "the yellow-wheeled buggy and the matched team of bays from the livery stable." Some were pleased for her because she had no one; her controlling, aristocratic father had died years before, leaving her to live in a house once acknowledged to be on the finest street in town. "The big, squarish frame house had once been white, decorated with cupolas, spires, and scrolled balconies, but with the passing of time and lack of repair, the house lifted its stubborn and coquettish decay above the cotton wagons and the gasoline pumps—an eyesore among eyesores."

The ladies in the town said, "'Of course a Grierson would not think seriously of a Northerner, a day laborer,'" but soon the whispering began in earnest. "'Do you suppose it's really so?' they said to one another. 'Of course it is.'"

When the town learned Miss Emily had "been to the jeweler's and ordered a man's toilet set in silver, with the letters H. B. on each piece and then two days later learned she had bought a complete outfit of men's clothing, including a nightshirt, they said, 'They are married.'" Oddly, however, shortly after these purchases, Homer Barron was never seen again. His disappearance coincided with Miss Emily's purchase of arsenic at the pharmacy. The label read "for rats." Shortly after that purchase Miss Emily also disappeared. Occasionally she could be seen looking out of an upstairs window like the time the townsmen skulked about the foundations of her house at midnight sprinkling lime in an effort to rid the street of an unaccountably bad smell; but otherwise, she was rarely seen.

When ultimately she died at the age of seventy-four, the towns-people felt bad; no one even knew she was sick. "She died in one of the downstairs rooms in a heavy walnut bed with a curtain, her iron-gray head propped on a pillow yellow and moldy with age and lack of sunlight."

After the funeral, the visiting cousins who came from Alabama to bury Miss Emily opened the house to a few officials who needed to examine the premises and to prepare the property for sale. They seemed to know there was one room in "that region above stairs which no one had seen in forty years, and would have to be forced open."

The story concludes with these chilling paragraphs:

The violence of breaking down the door seemed to fill this room with pervading dust. A thin, acrid pall as of the tomb seemed to lie everywhere upon this room decked and furnished as a bridal suite. Upon the dressing table was a delicate array of crystal and the man's toilet things backed with tarnished silver, silver so tarnished that the monogram was obscured. Among them lay a collar and tie, as if they had just been removed, which, lifted, left upon the surface, a pale crescent in the dust. Upon a chair hung the suit, carefully folded; beneath it the two mute shoes and the discarded socks.

The man himself lay in the bed.

For a long while we just stood there, looking down at the profound and fleshless grin. The body had apparently once lain in the attitude of an embrace. . . . What was left of him rotted beneath what was left of the nightshirt, had become inextricable from the bed in which he lay; and upon him and upon the pillow beside him lay that even coating of the patient and abiding dust.

Then we noticed that in the second pillow was the indention of a head. One of us lifted something from it, and leaning forward, that faint and invisible dust dry and acrid to the nostrils, we saw a long strand of iron-gray hair.

If the story is unfamiliar to you, you may be muttering to yourself, "Well, surely . . . you don't mean . . . well, that's disgusting! That strand of iron-gray hair on the adjoining pillow . . . you mean . . . was she . . . did she . . . well, talk about sick!"

Yes, it is indeed sick. Miss Emily was not gray when she poisoned Homer with arsenic. He had been in the upstairs bedroom for many years. The horrifying realization that she had been lying with Homer's corpse for all that time raises the obvious question, "Why?"

On the literal level Miss Emily had been jilted by Homer (you don't jilt a Grierson). She had also intended to spend the rest of her life with him . . . and so she did. On the figurative level, Miss Emily is thought to represent the South—an entire society that lived with a dead but unburied past. The South's careful attempts to maintain old traditions and ways of thinking, though no longer effective, were clung to with a tenacity and refusal to accept change much as Miss Emily refused to bury Homer.

On a more personal level, I think Miss Emily represents many of us. We too are living with a dead but unburied past. Unhealthy guilt and shame, those left-of-the-zipper secrets and addictions from which we can be healed, the anger that secretes shooting poison, our fear-based lying, and that devastating insecurity which encourages the use of fake ID—all need to be given a funeral. They are dead and we need to bury them.

Burying the Dead

How can I say that our left-of-the-zipper issues are dead when they feel so alive? We have given those issues power by believing the lies that we are powerless. We are not powerless. We can experience healing, release, and victory over those issues if we will let them go and quit lying down and embracing them because they're familiar. In a perverse way we are attached to those corpses. They have become a part of our identity.

The second chapter of Ephesians teaches that we are no longer dead in trespasses and sin . . . we have been made alive through Christ and raised from the dead. We are raised up to salvation; we are raised up to victorious living. We experience victory when through Him we are enabled to bury what is already dead. What's dead? Our left-of-the-zipper issues! To the degree they are sin, they're forgiven; to the degree they're rooted in shame, they represent potential healing and overcoming. Either way, a celebration is in order! Jesus said He came that we might have life . . . not death. Life and victory are from Him.

But let's go back over all this in slow motion. We have a funeral to plan, and we need to make sure we understand why everything's dead before we pick out the caskets. To begin with, the traumas we've discussed and the shame and deep sense of unworthiness that produce some of our behaviors are not issues of sin. They come under the category of developmental and environmental hurt. I hope the encouragement, not only to get help, but also the guidance on how to seek help has been motivating to you. I also hope you recognize the power the Holy Spirit promises you, which enables you to bury the past (not as in denial, but as in six feet under) and empowers you to exist in a living, forgiven present.

However, many of the issues we've discussed have a sin root, and it's the understanding of how that sin is to be seen as dead and buried that most moves my heart. In fact, that understanding revolutionized my thinking and spiritual life more than thirty years ago.

In this discussion the apostle Paul is our teacher as well as example, so we're going to do a bit of exciting Bible study here. Romans 6:4 states, "We were therefore buried with him through baptism into death in order that, just as Christ was raised from the dead through the glory of the Father, we too may live a new life" (NIV). Paul is saying that Jesus died, He was buried, and He was raised again. Our old lives with their addictions, anger, lying, and other sins have been crucified with Christ; they have been put to death. When we accept Christ as Savior, we put to death the old life, the corrupt human nature that so frequently troubles us. That nature is dead and buried, Paul proclaims. So just as Christ came out of the tomb with a new power for life, we too, because we received Him and His resurrection power into our innermost being, have a new power for life. That power is given to us through the Holy Spirit.

Paul also says in verse 5, "If we have been united with him like this in his death, we will certainly also be united with him in his resurrection" (NIV). We as Christians identify with Christ's death, but we also identify with His resurrection. That resurrection power enables us to live in new-ness of life; that resurrection power enables us to bury our dead.

Then Paul says something in Romans 6:6 that is what we're looking for: "For we know that our old self was crucified with him so that the body of sin might be done away with" (NIV). There's the proof you have that our sin issues are dead and need to be buried. But read this again: " . . . that the body of sin might be done away with." What exactly does Paul mean by "body of sin"? What body? My body . . . your body? Prepare yourself: The following explanation for that line may sound worse than Miss Emily lying with the dead Homer.

Behavior versus Identity

There was, in the ancient world, a particular punishment used on occa-sion for persons guilty of murder. The convicted murderer was sen-tenced to have the corpse of his victim tied to his back, so that wherever he went and whatever he did, he was never separated from the rotting flesh of the one whose life he had taken. Some biblical scholars have said this may be what Paul had in mind when he used the phrase "body of sin." We carry our own foul-smelling, corrupt sin identity on our back until we are set free from it when we put our faith in Christ. At that point the corpse drops and is buried immediately. We then have a new identity and are free of the burden of carting a corpse; we are free of the smell that corpse produced! Great news!

"Yes," you say, "but dead, buried, or living, I still have a problem with sin!" So do I; so do we all. Let's go back to Paul. You will remem-ber the familiar struggle with his "two selves" recorded in Romans 7:15, 19: "For that which I am doing, I do not understand; for I am not practicing what I would like to do, but I am doing the very thing I hate. . . . For the good that I wish, I do not do; but I practice the very evil that I do not wish" (NASB).

Paul wrote this after his Damascus Road conversion. He was a genuine believer in Jesus when he wrote those words. Paul, with all his being, wanted to banish evil impulses from his life . . . and yet he struggled. Many believers don't seem to realize that, like Paul, there is within each of us a magnetic pull toward sinful behavior. We were born with that pull, and even as genuine, sincere, forgiven believers in Jesus, we will die with that pull.

Consider, however, the distinction between us as believers with the magnetic pull toward sin and nonbelievers. The nonbeliever likes his sin, sees no reason to discontinue his sin, and rarely feels guilt about his sin. The Holy Spirit–occupied believer, on the other hand, is miserable in his sin. There may be pleasure in the behavior, but there is also the sting of guilt and a sense of spiritual disconnection that is overwhelming. If, when you sin, you do not feel remorse, guilt, or any desire to repent, I question if the Spirit of God lives within you. Remember "religious" Stanley in chapter 10 who thought he was a believer and then was shocked to experience his first surge of true conviction and guilt when he heard the phrase "you will know them by their fruits"? Just because you sin does not mean you never became a Christian. If you sin and feel miserable about it, go stand next to Paul. I'll be there right beside you.

Now, while we're there, let's read a statement that could sound like an incredibly creative bit of blame shifting. Paul says in Romans 7:16–17, "But if I do the very thing I do not wish to do, . . . no longer am I the one doing it, but sin which indwells me" (NASB). This almost sounds like the old "the-devil-made-me-do-it" excuse. But Paul is not denying personal responsibility here, although it almost sounds like it. What he's saying is that the real me, the new buried and resurrected me, the person I am because of Jesus, is not the one doing the sin. So who is? The old self who has been put to death with Christ! Now hang on; here's the explanation for those seemingly contradictory comments.

Paul says in Romans 7:18, "I know that nothing good lives in me, that is, in my sinful nature" (NIV). So Paul knows something good dwells within him: God the Holy Spirit dwells within him, transforming his very nature. But there is nothing good dwelling in his sin nature. So in verse 23, Paul makes a distinction between the innermost self and the other self, which is his sin nature: "But I see another law at work in the members of my body, waging war against the law of my mind and making me a prisoner of the law of sin at work within my members" (NIV).

So here's the liberating truth: The sinning Christian is not evil! There is something evil within the Christian person that is doing the sinning, but the sin nature was killed and buried. The sin tendency still exists and causes war within our beings, but it is crucial to understand that we and the sin are not one and the same. We have been cleansed and forgiven of all sin. The sinful identity is not ours any longer. Our new identity is that of one made perfect in spite of the power of sin that affects us. Our identity is in Jesus.

Admittedly, this is a very difficult truth to grasp. Perhaps this illustration will help. Although I had my silicone breast implants removed last year, my body still has toxic poison creeping sluggishly through its system. I continue to have some health challenges as a result; apparently I always will. I know the silicone is there because I can see it on a sonogram and I can feel its effects in my body. But the reality is there is nothing wrong with me . . . I am a redeemed and valuable child of God. There is, however, something wrong *in* me, wrong in my body. I will feel the effects of what is wrong in my body until the day I die. The same is true of sin in me. I will always feel its presence and pull, but I am not that sin; I am a reborn child of God who is dead to sin.

Why is it crucial for us to grasp the distinction between the sin nature that is dead and deserves a burial and that part of us which will always be drawn to sin as long as we live? To answer that question, let's assume we know a youth pastor named Toby who is addicted to pornography. Toby needs to know that even though his marriage, ministry, and reputation may soon be in jeopardy (when he's caught, and he will be . . . God will see to that, not because he's a "gotcha

God," but because he's a healing God), if Toby has received Christ as his Savior, that Savior did not walk away from Toby or his sin. Toby's spiritual identity is still secure in Christ. This is an important truth for Toby to rest in when he seeks rehabilitation and healing. Jesus did not come only to free Toby from the *penalty* of sin, but also to free him from the *power* of sin. This process of liberation may include a twelve-step program, therapy, and pastoral accountability sessions. God uses others in partnership with His goal to free His people. However He orchestrates it, the goal is emancipation from the toxic tenants that rule the left side of the heart.

Leaving the Dead Buried

So now it's time to bury what is dead. What's the first step? To agree with the teaching of Scripture, which states we are no longer dead in our sins, but alive in Jesus. That being true, we haul out everything to the left of the zipper, declare it dead, and in the name of Him who put it to death, thank Jesus that it is not allowed any more power over us.

Perhaps you would benefit from a tangible, literal exercise of burying your left-of-the-zipper issues. If so, you could conduct an actual funeral for all those creeps living to the left. You can not only evict them, you can bury them six feet under as well! So, if you're game, here's what you can do:

1. Write on a piece of paper one left-hearted issue (no group burials). Since you may be conducting a service for several toxic tenants, you may have a number of little "caskets."

2. Place that piece of paper upon which your issue is written in a small container (match box, raisin box, etc.) and close it.

3. Holding it in your hands, lift the box up to the Father and pray, "'O God, who declares me innocent' [Psalm 4:1 NLT], I

thank You for the forgiveness of this issue and I thank You it is a dead issue."

4. Find a spot behind a shrub (not your neighbor's), dig a deep hole, and place the box in it.

5. Fill in the hole with dirt and walk away.

As mildly ludicrous as this exercise may sound, I guarantee from this point on that when the toxic tenants you've buried spring to your mind to tempt you, accuse you, or demean you, you will see in your mind the burial site and you will remember what it felt like to bury them.

The second step in leaving the dead behind is to accept the tug of sin that will always be with us. We rarely experience victory by struggling against the sin itself. We experience victory by setting our minds on Jesus. Colossians 3:1–3 says, "If then you have been raised up with Christ, keep seeking the things above, where Christ is, seated at the right hand of God. Set your mind on the things above, not on the things that are on earth. For you have died and your life is hidden with Christ in God" (NASB).

How do we set our minds on things above? Through listening to praise music, memorizing and meditating on Scripture, spending quality time with other Christians and like-minded seekers who choose victory and not defeat, and by choosing an environment that is conducive to building our faith-walk with Jesus.

Finally, realize that concentrating on overcoming sin only causes us to see the sin. We need to concentrate instead on Jesus; He, not the sin, is our focus. The value of understanding that we have an alive and active sin pull coupled with a dead sin nature comes into play here. When we concentrate on that part of ourselves which is redeemed, cleansed, forgiven, and made new because of Jesus, we stop focusing on sin and refocus on Him. How we think and where we choose to focus are key.

Paul wraps it up beautifully in Romans 8:5–6: "Those who are according to the flesh set their minds on the things of the flesh, but those who are according to the Spirit, the things of the Spirit. For the mind set on the flesh is death, but the mind set on the Spirit is life and peace" (NASB).

Is it yet another seeming paradox to say that our determination, will power, or self-discipline to live above the pull of sin is ineffective and doomed to fail when we stress we can choose how we think and where we focus? No, because God invites our participation, but He is ultimately the One who enables. He uses the earthly aids we seek—therapy, twelve-step programs, pastoral accountability—for His purpose, which is to free us and enable us to leave our dead buried. But we are power-less over sin if we are not in partnership with Him because it is He and He alone who gives us the power to overcome.

Out with the Old, In with the New

So, now what do we do with the zipper? I said in chapter 1 that I have found the zipper a handy construct to use in seeing more clearly how I may be disowning parts of my being—how I kick those disowned parts of myself into the shadowy darkness of denial, shame, or guilt to thrive on the zipper's left. To the degree the zipper keeps me current in focusing on how and when I do that, the zipper may continue to be a useful tool. In other words, the zipper keeps me informed, and as a result, I can spring into action when I catch myself doing the zipper-kick.

However, if I truly understand the teaching that those left-of-the-zipper issues are not me, that they are dead and have been buried, then what is the function of the zipper? Should the zipper be buried too?

Wouldn't it be great if each of us could live in recognition of human challenges and propensities to sin without having to wall those challenges and propensities off into shame-producing divisions? If Jesus walks freely on both sides of our heart, never even noting the sides, couldn't we do the same? What would enable us to stroll our soul's property as freely as He does? The only thing that would make this possible is to see ourselves as He does. And He sees us as whole, perfect creations. The divine mystery here is that in seeing us as perfect, He also sees when He wants to continue perfecting us into His image.

Those thoughts bump against the ceiling of my brain, causing me to realize yet again that His plan and His person are too big to fit the dimensions of my finite mind. Therefore, I'll try to follow His example and not be put off by my "stuff" any more than He is. That being the case, I have a strong suspicion I won't be needing the zipper after all. (Wonder what size box I should look for to bury it in?)

May I suggest now that you join me in living in the freeing wholeness Jesus promises to anyone who believes in Him and invites Him to dwell within their sin-stained heart? His sacrificial death cleanses us and makes us white as snow. So change the sheets, open the windows, and breathe in the clean, fresh, invigorating air of new life and overcoming victory!

Chat Room Possibilities

1. Can you pinpoint issues that you have refused to bury? Do you derive some sort of gratification in keeping them above ground? What is that gratification?

2. What is your response to Paul's teaching that our old sin nature is dead and buried when our present sin nature appears to be alive and well? How do you deal with that seeming conflict?

3. How and when has the indwelling power of the Holy Spirit enabled you to give dead issues a burial?

4. If you have never given a burial for those issues, how do you plan to do so?

5. Do you truly believe that you as a believer are without condemnation, or do you have some yeah buts with Romans 8:1?

Notes

CHAPTER 6

1. Paul Tournier, quoted in Lewis B. Smedes, *Shame and Grace* (Grand Rapids: Zondervan, 1993), 77.

2. Charles Swindoll, *Grace Awakening* (Nashville: Word, 1990), 46.

CHAPTER 8

1. Norvel Young, *Loving Lights Shining Stars* (West Monroe, La.: Howard Publishing, 1997), 9.

CHAPTER 10

1. Paul Dietz, "Voices from the Cell," *Time,* 28 May 2001, 33.

2. Neil Clark Warren, *Make Anger Your Ally* (New York: Doubleday, 1983), 111.

CHAPTER 11

1. Christine J. Gardner, "Tangled in the Worst of the Web," *Christianity Today,* March 2001, 42.

CHAPTER 12

1. Archibald Hart, Catherine Hart Weber, and Debra Taylor, *Secrets of Eve* (Nashville: Word, 1998), 35.

CHAPTER 13

1. Henri Nouwen, *The Road to Daybreak: A Spiritual Journey* (New York: Doubleday, 1988), 29.

CHAPTER 14

1. Simon Wiesenthal, *The Sunflower* (New York: Schocken Books, 1988), 97.

CHAPTER 15

1. Henri Nouwen, *Life of the Beloved* (New York: Crossroad Publishing, 1992), 27.

Acknowledgments

I want to thank W Publishing Group for its patience and incredible kindness as the due date for this book's completion came and went. While I tended to unexpected health issues for nearly a year, the only words I heard from W were those of encouragement coupled with periodic flower deliveries and prayers for God's healing. Laura Kendall and Debbie Wickwire will forever live in my heart as angels of mercy.

My thanks also to my incomparable editor, Traci Mullins, who brought order to structural chaos and clarity to verbal obscurity. Your skills are priceless; I deeply appreciate you.

My dear "porch pals" of Women of Faith, Luci Swindoll, Patsy Clairmont, Barbara Johnson, Thelma Wells, and Sheila Walsh, gave invaluable input as I cornered them with inappropriately probing questions like, "Do you ever lie? Do you have secrets I might share with the world? How forthcoming ought one to be about past sexual issues with one's husband?" etc., etc., etc.

Sharon Barnes, my wonderful friend and prayer partner, offered fervent prayer for my body and consistent enthusiasm for this book. I owe her more than lunch.

In it all, God continues to exhibit a flair, style, and faithfulness that astounds me, and for which I am grateful.

Made in the USA
Lexington, KY
28 October 2014